CROSSROADS
OF FREEDOM

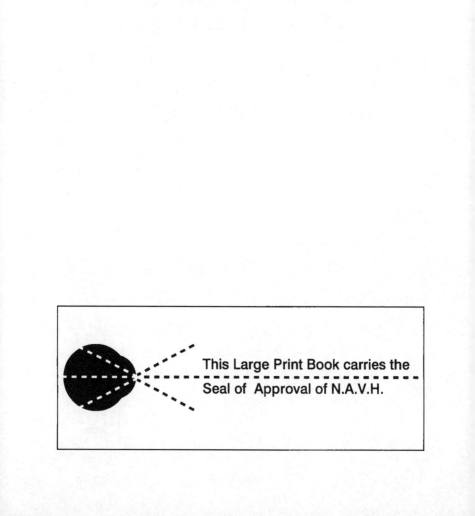

This Large Print Book carries the
Seal of Approval of N.A.V.H.

Crossroads
of Freedom

ANTIETAM

James M. McPherson

Thorndike Press • Waterville, Maine

Published in 2002 by arrangement with
Oxford University Press, Inc.

Thorndike Press Large Print American History Series.

The tree indicium is a trademark of Thorndike Press.

The text of this Large Print edition is unabridged.
Other aspects of the book may vary from the original edition.

Set in 16 pt. Plantin.

Printed in the United States on permanent paper.

Library of Congress Cataloging-in-Publication Data

McPherson, James M.
    Crossroads of freedom : Antietam / James M.
McPherson.
        p. cm.
    Includes bibliographical references (p. 326)
    ISBN 0-7862-4909-9 (lg. print : hc : alk. paper)
    1. Antietam, Battle of, Md., 1862. 2. Large type books.
I. Title.
E474.65 .M48 2002b
    973.7′336—dc21   2002035861

To Gwynne
and to her bronze friend,
Mr. Lincoln

PIVOTAL MOMENTS
IN AMERICAN HISTORY

Series Editors

David Hackett Fischer
James M. McPherson

James T. Patterson
Brown v. Board of Education:
A Civil Rights Milestone and
Its Troubled Legacy

Maury Klein
Rainbow's End:
The Crash of 1929

Contents

Maps

Editor's Note

This volume is part of a new series called Pivotal Moments in American History. Our purpose is to encourage interest in problems of historical contingency.

Scholars in many disciplines have been moving in this direction, and they have done so in different ways. A leading example is James McPherson's *Battle Cry of Freedom*, a general history of the Civil War that centers on "the dimension of contingency," in the sense of "turning points," when the war "might have gone altogether differently." Another is Stephen Jay Gould's *Wonderful Life: The Burgess Shale Fossils and the Nature of History*, which constructs a new model of natural history on "historical contingency" as small, unpredictable events that shaped the course of evolution. A third is my book *Paul Revere's Ride*, which is about "contingency" in yet another meaning of "people making choices, and choices making a difference." The logo for this series is one of the lanterns in the Old North Church.

Ideas of contingency are drawing more attention in historical scholarship, for several reasons. They offer a way forward, beyond the "old political history" and the "new social and cultural history," by a reunion of process and event. They also restore a lost element of narrative tension to historical writing. A concept of contingency makes history more teachable and learnable, more readable and writable, more important and even urgent in our thinking about the world, and most of all more true to itself.

James McPherson's *Crossroads of Freedom* is a model of what might be done with this approach. The book is about the battle of Antietam (to Southerners, Sharpsburg), a great and terrible event that made September 17, 1862, the bloodiest day in American history. Much of the book is about small events such as Lee's lost Special Orders No. 191, which fell into McClellan's hands at an opportune moment. James McPherson speculates about that chance happening in a fresh and thoughtful way, by asking what might have happened if McClellan's Special Orders had fallen into Lee's hands. Counterfactual questions are heuristically useful as what the Germans call thought experiments.

But counterfactual questions and reductive explanations are not what this book is mainly about. This is a history of contingency in a larger spirit and a different key. It takes a long view of its subject and sets the battle firmly in the context of large historical processes. This is also an idea of historical change not as a single transforming event, but as a web of contingencies.

The book is also a model in another way. In a work of large purpose, where particular details make a difference, historians must get the small things right. The quality of James McPherson's scholarship is an example to us all in that respect, more so than one might realize from a quick and easy reading. Its narrative is so fluent that a reader might miss the author's unrivaled command of the subject, his mastery of the materials, his meticulous attention to matters of substance and detail, and his uncompromising integrity in a long career of research and reflection on the American Civil War.

In all of these ways, this book is a model of large importance for the study of the past and a way forward for scholarship in the future. I hope that you, the reader, will think so too.

David Hackett Fischer

Preface

The meaning of freedom was central to the meaning of the American Civil War. Freedom, or liberty, has been a contested issue through all of American history. "We all declare for liberty," said Abraham Lincoln during the war, "but in using the same *word* we do not all mean the same *thing*." Three definitions of freedom struggled for dominance from 1861 to 1865. The Confederacy, said its President Jefferson Davis, was "forced to take up arms to vindicate the political rights, the freedom, equality, and State sovereignty which were the heritage purchased by the blood of our revolutionary sires." But Lincoln insisted that an independent Confederacy would destroy the nation established by those revolutionary sires as the "last best hope" for the preservation of republican freedom. "We must settle this question now," said Lincoln a month after the outbreak of war, "whether in a free government the minority have the right to break up the government whenever they choose."

Neither the Union nor Confederacy at first included the emancipation of four million slaves in its definition of the freedoms for which each side fought. Indeed, the Confederate states had seceded from the Union to escape the perceived threat posed by Lincoln's election to the survival of slavery. "That *perfect* liberty they sigh for," said Lincoln, "is the liberty of making slaves of other people." Yet Lincoln in 1861 did not embrace the goal of freedom for slaves in this war for Union. But many of the slaves did. By escaping to Union lines they voted with their feet for liberty. They took the first steps toward expanding the North's definition of the freedom for which it fought to include their freedom.

In the spring of 1862, however, a succession of Northern naval and military victories seemed to foretell imminent defeat of the Confederacy and restoration of "the Union as it was" — a Union with slavery. But Southern counteroffensives in the summer of 1862 reversed the momentum of war and by September of that year brought the Confederacy to the brink of military victory and of diplomatic recognition of its independent nationhood by foreign powers. Ironically, this Confederate success convinced Lincoln to "take off the kid gloves" in dealing with slavery and to adopt emancipation as a means of weakening the Confederacy and strengthening the Union cause.

These competing visions of freedom rushed toward a collision in September 1862 as General Robert E. Lee's Army of Northern Virginia invaded Maryland seeking a war-winning victory over the Army of the Potomac commanded by General George B. McClellan. The tremendous shock of that collision in the battle of Antietam near the village of Sharpsburg changed the course of the war. Union victory at Antietam, limited though it was, arrested Southern military momentum, forestalled foreign recognition of the Confederacy, reversed a disastrous decline in the morale of Northern soldiers and civilians, and offered Lincoln the opportunity to issue a proclamation of emancipation. In a war with several crucial turning points, the battle of Antietam was the pivotal moment for the most crucial of them all. This book provides a map to guide readers to that crossroads of freedom at Sharpsburg.

James M. McPherson
Princeton, New Jersey

14

Louisiana soldiers killed on the morning of September 17 along the fence bordering the Hagerstown Pike just south of the famous Cornfield at Antietam, photographed on September 19 by Alexander Gardner. (Library of Congress)

Confederate soldiers killed near the Dunkard church on the morning of September 17, photographed two days later by Alexander Gardner. (Library of Congress)

Introduction

Death in September

Despite the ghastly events of September 11, 2001, another September day 139 years earlier remains the bloodiest single day in American history. The 6,300 to 6,500 Union and Confederate soldiers killed and mortally wounded near the Maryland village of Sharpsburg on September 17, 1862, were more than twice the number of fatalities suffered in the terrorist attacks on the World Trade Center and the Pentagon on September 11, 2001.[1] Another 15,000 men wounded in the battle of Antietam would recover, but many of them would never again walk on two legs or work with two arms. The number of casualties at Antietam was four times greater than American casualties at the Normandy beaches on June 6, 1944. More American soldiers died at Sharpsburg (the Confederate name for the battle) than died in combat in all the other wars fought by this country in the nineteenth century *combined:* the War of 1812, the Mexican–American War, the Spanish–American War, and all the Indian wars.

Even at the distance of 140 years, such statistics send a shiver down one's spine. Yet these cold facts pale in comparison with descriptions of the battlefield by participants and witnesses — mainly Northerners, because the Confederate Army of Northern Virginia retreated across the Potomac River on the night of September 18–19, leaving most of their dead and many wounded to be buried or treated by the Union Army of the Potomac. "I was on the battlefield yesterday where we were engaged," wrote a Union artillery officer on September 19, "and the dead rebels strewed the ground and in some places were on top of each other. Two hundred dead could be counted in one small field." Another Northern officer counted "hundreds of dead bodies lying in rows and in piles . . . looking the picture of all that is sickening, harrowing, horrible. O what a terrible sight!"[2] A Union lieutenant in charge of a burial party where his regiment (57th New York) fought described the dead "in every state of mutilation, sans arms, sans legs, heads, and intestines, and in greater number than on any field we have seen before." A local resident who rode over the battlefield on September 19 traced the Confederate line "by the dead lying along it as they fell. . . . The line I suppose was a mile long or more. . . . Down in the corn field I saw a man with a hole in his belly about as big as a hat and about a quart of dark-looking maggots working away."[3]

The most concentrated carnage took place in a sunken farm road in the center of the Confederate line, known ever after as Bloody Lane. A Union lieutenant colonel whose New York regiment was in the thick of the fighting at Bloody Lane described the scene there after the battle: "In the road the dead covered the ground. It seemed, as I rode along, that it was the Valley of Death. I think that in the space of less than ten acres, lay the bodies of a thousand dead men and as many more wounded." An enlisted man in this regiment who had captured a Confederate battle flag in the sunken road wrote in his diary on September 19: "Today I was given detaile to burry the Dead Rebels, just where I captured the flag at 2:00 pm of the 17th. 12 lengths of fence being counted off for my station & in 10 rods [55 yards] we have piled and burried 264 . . . &

4 Detailes has been obliged to do likewise, it was a Sight I never want to encounter again." A lieutenant in the 14th Connecticut, which also fought at Bloody Lane, described "hundreds of horses too, all mangled and putrefying, scattered everywhere."[4]

By September 24 the bodies were buried and some of the horses had been dragged into piles, doused with coal oil, and burned. But the battlefield still presented a scene from hell, as described by an official of the United States Sanitary Commission who had brought medical supplies for the wounded. "No words can convey" the "utter devastation and ruin," he wrote, but he tried to find words anyway. "For four miles in length, and nearly half a mile in width, the ground is strewn with . . . hats, caps, clothing, canteens, knapsacks, shells and shot." Scattered around were "long mounds of earth, where, underneath, five thousand men, wrapped in their blankets, were laid side by side. . . . Visit a battlefield and see what a victory costs!"[5]

A week after the battle a newspaper in Hagerstown (a dozen miles from the battlefield) reported that in an area of seventy-five square miles "wounded and dying soldiers are to be found in every neighborhood and in nearly every house. . . . The whole region of country between Boonsboro and Sharpsburg is one vast hospital" and "nearly the whole population" were trying to take care of the wounded. This was no pleasant task. "The odor from the battlefield and the hospitals is almost insupportable," wrote the surgeon of a New Hampshire regiment. "No one can begin to estimate the amount of agony after a great battle. . . . The poor mutilated soldiers that yet have life and sensation make a most horrid picture."[6]

Months after the battle, Sharpsburg continued to disgorge new forms of hideousness. During Robert E. Lee's invasion of Pennsylvania in June 1863, which culminated in the battle of Gettysburg, part of his army marched over the Antietam battlefield. A private in the 23rd Virginia described "the most horrible sights that my eyes ever beheld," hundreds of bodies that had been buried in shallow graves the previous September "just lying on top of the ground with a little dirt throwed over them and the hogs rooting them out of the ground and eating them and others lying on top of the ground with the flesh picked off and their bones bleaching."[7]

Major Rufus Dawes of the 6th Wisconsin, a regiment in the famous Iron Brigade, fought through the war in most of the Eastern theater's deadliest battles: Second Bull Run, Fredericksburg, Gettysburg, the Wilderness, Spotsylvania, and the battles around Petersburg as well as at Antietam. Looking back after the war, he wrote that Antietam "surpassed all in manifest evidence of slaughter." Many other veterans on both sides echoed this conclusion. A survey of thousands of surviving Union and Confederate soldiers after the war found that for an extraordinary number of them, no matter how many other battles they had fought, Antietam stood out as the worst.[8]

Stark memories of Antietam haunted many for the rest of their days. A private in the 1st Delaware, which suffered 230 casualties in the battle, recalled a Union soldier "stumbling around with both eyes shot out, begging someone 'for the love of God' to put an end to his misery." A nearby lieutenant asked him if he really meant what he said. "Oh yes," the blinded soldier replied. "I cannot possibly live, and my agony is unendurable." Without another word the lieutenant drew his revolver, "placed it to the victim's right ear, turned away his head, and pulled the trigger. A half-wheel, a convulsive gasp, and one more unfortunate had passed over to the silent majority. 'It was better thus,' said the lieutenant, replacing his pistol and turning toward [me], 'for the poor fellow could —' Just then a solid shot took the lieutenant's head off."[9]

The shock of such scenes caused psychiatric casualties among even the most hardened and experienced soldiers. Colonel William R. Lee of the elite 20th Massachusetts, who had gone through a half-dozen previous battles without losing his poise, rode away from his regiment the morning after Antietam without telling anyone and was later found, according to one of his subordinates, "without a cent in his pocket, without anything to eat or drink, without having changed his clothes for 4 weeks, during all which time he had this horrible diarrhea. . . . He was just like a little child wandering away from home."[10]

Soldiers who wrote home to family members eager to hear about their experiences told them that they could not begin to depict the enormity of it. "Words are inadequate to portray the scene," wrote one. "I will not attempt to tell you of it," inscribed another.[11] For Northern civilians who wanted to see something of the "ghastly spectacle" without actually going there, an opportunity soon presented itself. Within two days of the battle, Northern photographers Alexander Gardner and James Gibson arrived at Antietam and began taking pictures. For the first time in history, the graphic and grisly sight of bloated corpses killed in action could be seen by those who never came close to the battlefield. Gardner and Gibson worked for Mathew Brady, whose studio in New York City exhibited the photographs a month after the battle.

The unburied soldiers in these photographs were nearly all Confederates — probably because the Union dead were interred first, before Gardner and Gibson arrived, but perhaps also because pictures of Union dead might have had a dampening effect on Northern morale. In any event, a *New York Times* reporter who saw this exhibit on "The Dead of Antietam" wrote sympathetically of their Southern families whose grief invited empathy rather than enmity. "Mr. Brady has done something to bring home to us the terrible reality and earnestness of war," he informed readers of the *Times* on October 20, 1862. "If he has not brought bodies and laid them in our door-yards and along streets, he has done something very like it." But "there is one side of the picture that . . . has escaped photographic skill. It is the background of widows and orphans. . . . Homes have been made desolate, and the light of life in thousands of hearts has been quenched forever. All of this desolation imagination must paint — broken hearts cannot be photographed."

What had been accomplished by "all of this desolation"? The surgeon of a New Hampshire regiment, who remained in the vicinity of Sharpsburg for more than a month to treat the wounded, could find no answer to this question. "To the feeling man this war is truly a tragedy but to the thinking man it must appear a *madness*," he wrote. "We win a great victory. It goes through the country. The masses rejoice, but if all could see the thousands of poor, suffering, dieing men their rejoicing would turn to weeping. . . . I pray God may stop such infernal work — though perhaps he has sent it upon us for our sins. Great indeed must have been our sins if such is our punishment."[12]

A Massachusetts officer who fought at Antietam also was troubled to fathom its meaning. Robert Gould Shaw was a captain in the 2nd Massachusetts Infantry, one of the best Union regiments on the field. "Every battle makes me wish more and more that the war was over," Shaw wrote to his father four days after the carnage. "It seems almost as if nothing could justify a battle like that of the 17th, and the horrors inseparable from it."[13]

Shaw's next battle was the assault on Fort Wagner on July 18, 1863, in which he was killed at the head of the 54th Massachusetts, the first black regiment recruited in the North. His family believed that the courage Shaw and his men demonstrated in that battle justified his death. But Shaw's question about Antietam lingers; what could justify such slaughter and desolation as occurred there? Two men who would have agreed on little else answered that question in a similar way. From London, where he followed the American Civil War with close attention, Karl Marx wrote in October 1862 that Antietam "has decided the fate of the American Civil War." And looking back some years later, Colonel Walter H. Taylor of Robert E. Lee's wartime staff described Sharpsburg as the decisive "event of the war."[14]

Many soldiers who fought there would have agreed that Antietam was "the event" that decided "the fate of the American

Civil War." They believed that the destiny of their respective nations — the United States and the Confederate States — rested on the outcome of this battle. They fought as if there would be no tomorrow. That was why for so many of them there *was* no tomorrow. For the others, of course, there were many more tomorrows and much more bloodshed as the war continued for two and one-half years after Antietam.

No single battle decided the outcome of the Civil War. Several turning points brought reversals of an apparently inexorable momentum toward victory by one side and then the other during the war. Two such pivotal moments occurred in the year that preceded Antietam. Union naval and military victories in the early months of 1862 blunted previous Southern triumphs and brought the Confederacy almost to its knees. But Southern counteroffensives in the summer turned the war around. When the Army of Northern Virginia crossed the Potomac River into Maryland in September 1862, the Confederacy appeared to be on the brink of victory. Antietam shattered that momentum. Never again did Southern armies come so close to conquering a peace for an independent Confederacy as they did in September 1862. Even though the war continued and the Confederacy again approached success on later occasions, Antietam was arguably, as Karl Marx and Walter Taylor believed, *the* event of the war. To understand why, we must turn back the clock to the first year of the conflict.

One

The Pendulum of War
1861–1862

In most civil wars or revolutions, the insurrectionary army must fight to gain control of land, or government, or both. In the American Civil War, however, the eleven states of the Confederacy established a functioning government at Richmond in May 1861 with its armies in control of virtually all of the 750,000 square miles that constituted its national territory. To "win" the war that began with Confederate seizure of Fort Sumter, the South needed only to defend what it already possessed by repelling enemy invasions and wearing out the will of the Northern people to carry on the war.

By contrast, if President Abraham Lincoln wished to achieve his war aims of preserving the United States as a whole nation — a Union of *all* the states — his armies would have to invade the Confederacy, defeat its armies, conquer and occupy its territory, and destroy its government. To many contemporary observers, this task appeared impossible. Events in 1861 did nothing to alter that appearance. Union arms did win some victories that year, to be sure. The navy captured bases for its blockade fleets along the coasts of North and South Carolina. Northern troops secured control of most parts of the crucial border states of Missouri, Kentucky, and Maryland — though they lost two battles in Missouri. Union forces also drove small Confederate armies out of western Virginia, paving the way for later admission of West Virginia as a new Union state.

But the first drive "On to Richmond" had been stopped by a humiliating defeat along the banks of Bull Run in July 1861, and another Union thrust had met disaster at Balls Bluff on the Potomac River near Leesburg, Virginia, in October. Although Union forces held precarious toeholds around the Confederate perimeter in Virginia and along the south Atlantic coast, the Confederacy balanced these incursions by occupying the southern portions of Kentucky and Missouri. The Union naval blockade was not yet effective, and nine out of ten ships that ran the porous cordon of blockaders got through safely in 1861. At the end of that year the Confederacy stood proud and defiant.

Northern spirits had risen temporarily in November when a Union warship captured Confederate envoys James Mason and John Slidell from the British steamer *Trent*. This action, however, provoked a diplomatic crisis and potential war with Britain. Already embroiled in one war it seemed unable to win, the Lincoln administration could not risk a second one. The day after Christmas 1861 the U.S. government released Mason and Slidell, thereby averting war but also producing a feeling of letdown and shame in the North. This "*Trent* affair" had provoked a financial panic in the North. Banks briefly suspended specie payments (the backing of their notes with gold or silver). Secretary of the Treasury Salmon P. Chase found it difficult to sell bonds to finance the war.

All of this might have mattered little if military prospects had seemed more promising. After the defeat at Bull Run, Lincoln had called General George B. McClellan to take command of the Army of the Potomac. An energetic, talented officer only thirty-four years old, small of stature but great with an aura of destiny, McClellan enjoyed the adulation of the press and political leaders who hailed him as "the young Napoleon." At the age of nineteen, McClellan had graduated second in the West Point class of 1846. After distinguished service in the Mexican War, he compiled a good record in the regular army, winning a coveted appointment as a

"The Young Napoleon" George B. McClellan with his wife, Ellen, to whom he had written after he took command of the Army of the Potomac: "By some strange power of magic I have become the power of the land. God has placed a great work in my hands." (Library of Congress)

military observer with the British in the Crimean War. Promotion was slow in the peacetime army, however, and McClellan resigned in 1857 to become superintendent of first one and then a second Midwestern railroad. In this capacity his extraordinary organizational skills impressed everyone who came into contact with him, leading to a commission to organize Ohio regiments when war broke out in 1861. In June and July, McClellan led a small army to victories that secured Union control of much of the area that became West Virginia. This success brought the call to Washington and command of the Union's largest army after Bull Run.

McClellan cultivated his Napoleonic image. Possessing a remarkable charisma that bonded officers and men to his leadership, he organized and trained the Army of the Potomac into a large, well-disciplined fighting force. The soldiers' affection for McClellan became legendary. "You have no idea how the men brighten up now when I go among them," he wrote to his wife. "I never heard such yelling. . . . I can see every eye glisten."[1] McClellan seemed to be just what the North needed after the dispiriting defeat at Bull Run. When the aged, ailing Winfield Scott stepped down as general in chief on November 1, 1861, McClellan took over that post as well.

These were McClellan's honeymoon months with the Northern public. But as the fine autumn days slipped by and the Army of the Potomac did nothing to drive off Confederate outposts only a few miles from Washington, the honeymoon came to an end. McClellan's failings began to manifest themselves. He was a perfectionist in a profession where nothing could ever be perfect. His army was perpetually *almost* ready to move, but could not do so until the last horse was shoed and the last soldier fully equipped. McClellan was afraid to risk failure, so he risked nothing. He consistently overestimated the strength of enemy forces confronting him (sometimes by multiples of two or three) and used these faulty estimates as a reason for inaction. The caution and defensive-mindedness that McClellan infused into the Army of the Potomac persisted for almost three years, yielding the initiative to its adversary, commanded after May 1862 by the greatest risk-taker of all, Robert E. Lee.

McClellan's inaction plus his political convictions injected a dangerous poison into relations between the army and the government. McClellan made no secret of his disdain for abolitionists and Republicans in Congress and the press who began to criticize his inactivity in the fall of 1861. He also privately expressed contempt for Lincoln. In turn, some Republicans questioned whether McClellan, whose friends had been Democrats allied with the South before the war, really wanted to "strike the rebellion a blow." Even "Lincoln himself begins to think he smells a rat," wrote Postmaster-General Montgomery Blair in October.[2]

Suspicions of McClellan's loyalty to the Union cause were unfounded. But he and the officers whom he appointed to key positions were "soft" on slavery, and in a sense they were soft on the South as well. They did not want to fight the kind of war the radicals were beginning to demand — a war to destroy slavery and to reshape the South in the Northern free-soil, free-labor image. "Help me to dodge the nigger," McClellan wrote to an influential Democratic friend. "I am fighting to preserve the integrity of the Union. . . . To gain that end we cannot afford to mix up the negro question."[3] Mistrust between McClellan and his army on the one hand and the Republican administration and Congress on the other took root during this winter of

Northern discontent. They would bear bitter fruit.

To make matters worse, McClellan came down with typhoid fever just before Christmas. Lincoln's cup of woe seemed to run over. And news from the western theaters of war did nothing to cheer him up. General Henry W. Halleck commanded the Department of the Missouri with headquarters at St. Louis, and General Don Carlos Buell commanded the Department of the Ohio embracing the region between the Appalachians and the Cumberland River. Buell told Lincoln that the terrain and weather prevented him from moving against a Confederate force in East Tennessee. Halleck wrote the president on January 6 explaining why he could not attack the Confederate fortifications on the Mississippi at Columbus, Kentucky. On a copy of Halleck's letter, Lincoln wrote: "It is exceedingly discouraging. As everywhere else, nothing can be done." The president poured out his frustration to Quartermaster-General Montgomery Meigs. "General, what should I do? The people are impatient; Chase has no money and he tells me he can raise no more; the General of the Army has typhoid fever. The bottom is out of the tub. What shall I do?"[4]

These bleak January days turned out to be the darkness before a bright Northern dawn. From western Tennessee, coastal North Carolina, northern Arkansas, New Orleans, and Virginia itself came news of a succession of Union triumphs beginning in February 1862 that seemed to portend the imminent end of the Confederacy. Almost overnight the Northern mood vaulted from despondency to euphoria, and the Southern mood sank from confidence to despair. In February the Union Congress legislated the new greenback currency and Chase prepared to issue a new series of war bonds. Floated on the buoyant tide of victory, these measures patched the leaky hull of Union finances.

In the fall of 1861 an obscure Illinois brigadier general named Ulysses S. Grant took command of Union troops in Cairo, Illinois, at the confluence of the Ohio and Mississippi Rivers. He also sent troops to occupy Paducah and Smithland, Kentucky, where the Tennessee and Cumberland Rivers flow into the Ohio. These navigable rivers were highways of invasion into the Confederate heartland. The Southerners built Fort Henry on the Tennessee and Fort Donelson on the Cumberland where the two rivers flowed only twelve miles apart just south of the Kentucky–Tennessee border. Grasping the strategic importance of these forts, Grant planned a joint army–navy task force to capture them and open the rivers to Union gunboats.

These new vessels were formidable craft. Carrying thirteen big guns, drawing only six feet of water, with a sloping casemate sheathed in iron armor to protect hull and paddlewheels, the first four of these fearsome gunboats were ready to go by the end of January 1862. Grant urged Halleck to unleash him against Fort Henry. Unlike McClellan, who had known nothing but success in his life and was afraid to risk failure, Grant's experience of failure before the war made him willing to take risks, having little to lose. Backed by Flag Officer Andrew H. Foote, who commanded the gunboats, Grant persuaded Halleck to authorize the campaign.

Grant and Foote moved quickly. Badly sited on low ground, Fort Henry succumbed to the gunboat attack on February 6 before Grant's 15,000 soldiers could prevent the escape of most of the garrison to Fort Donelson. Almost without a pause, Grant and Foote closed in on Donelson and locked in its 14,000 defenders, outnumbered by Grant's 27,000, after sharp

USS *Cairo*, one of the ironclad Union gunboats that helped gain control of the Tennessee and Cumberland Rivers in 1862. During the initial campaign against Vicksburg the *Cairo* struck a mine on the Yazoo River on December 12, 1862, and went to the bottom. A century later its iron remains were raised and are on display at Vicksburg National Military Park. (Library of Congress)

fighting on both water and land February 14–15. Asked what terms of surrender he would offer the doomed garrison, Grant responded with a reply that made him famous: "No terms except an unconditional and immediate surrender can be accepted. I propose to move immediately upon your works." This ended discussion;

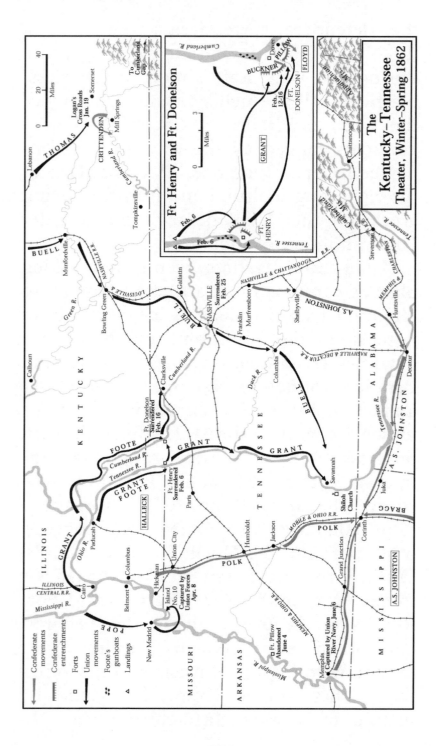

The Kentucky–Tennessee Theater, Winter–Spring 1862

Ft. Henry and Ft. Donelson

Confederate movements
Confederate entrenchments
Union movements
Foote's gunboats
Forts
Landings

the defenders surrendered, the first of three enemy armies Grant would capture during the war. Left almost defenseless, Nashville fell to Buell's advancing Army of the Ohio on February 25, while Union gunboats ranged all the way up the Tennessee River to Florence, Alabama. One of the richest agricultural and iron-producing areas of the Confederacy came under Union military occupation.

While these startling events were taking place, a campaign that attracted even more attention from the leading news media of both sides, the Richmond and New York newspapers, brought the Albemarle and Pamlico Sounds of North Carolina under Yankee control. An expeditionary force under General Ambrose E. Burnside supported by gunboats burst through Hatteras inlet and attacked Roanoke Island on February 7–8, captured most of its three thousand defenders, and fanned out to occupy other ports on the North Carolina sounds. During the next ten weeks Burnside's forces captured New Bern and Fort Macon at Beaufort, giving the Federals control of every North Carolina port except Wilmington. Burnside won a reputation that, unlike Grant, he would be unable to sustain through the war. To crown Union achievements during what turned out to be this winter of Southern discontent, a small Union army won a decisive victory at Pea Ridge in northwest Arkansas on March 7–8.

These events had a profound effect on home-front morale in both North and South. "Glorious News," "Great Victory," "Overwhelming Success," "Extreme Panic Among the Rebels," crowed the usually restrained *New York Times*. "It will not be long ere this huge and infernal revolt shall be crushed out. . . . The monster is already clutched and in his death struggle."[5] Horace Greeley's *New York Tribune*, the country's most influential Republican newspaper, was equally exuberant. "The marvelous change a few days have wrought in the aspect of national affairs is reflected in the faces of all men," declared the *Tribune* after the capture of Fort Donelson. "There is a glow of pride on every cheek" in the North. "Every blow tells fearfully against the rebellion. The rebels themselves are panic-stricken, or despondent. It requires no very far-seeing prophet to predict the end of this struggle."[6]

Not to be outdone, the independent but Democratic-leaning *New York Herald*, with the largest daily circulation of any American newspaper, announced after the capture of Fort Henry that "the gloomy night of our doubts and troubles is past." The war would be over and the Union restored "before the end of the month." Four days later the prediction was a less optimistic sixty days, and after additional Northern victories the *Herald* inexplicably postponed the end of the rebellion to the Fourth of July. With even more Union successes in March, however, the *Herald*'s optimism rose again: "We may now count on the final collapse of the vagrant government of Jeff. Davis before the 1st of May."[7]

This ebullience infected even the normally sober *Harper's Weekly*, which saw the Northern victories in February as "The Beginning of the End." "The night was very dark," acknowledged *Harper's* on March 22, "but the dawn is bright indeed, and surprisingly glorious. . . . There is not a point in the line of three thousand miles at which the rebels can make a stand."[8]

Like the *Tribune*, *Harper's* believed the Southern people to be "heart-broken, panic-stricken, and despairing at this turn of events."[9] Although wishful thinking exaggerated this claim, it was not far wrong. The shocking succession of defeats in February and March stunned Southerners. "The enemy have shown a daring that has taken us by surprise," admitted the *Richmond Enquirer*. With the fall of Fort Donelson "we have sustained another staggering blow," conceded the *Richmond Dispatch*, the newspaper with the largest circulation in the Confederacy. "Reverse after reverse comes in quick succession." A month later the *Dispatch* lamented that "we have nothing but disaster."[10]

Other newspapers agreed that the Confederacy had never known "an hour of deeper gloom or greater peril. . . . The crisis is too serious to mince words."[11] Two officials in the Confederate War Department whose diaries reflected public opinion in Richmond referred repeatedly to the "catalogue of disasters" in February. "There seems to me to be a more general feeling of despondency prevailing at this time than ever before."[12]

Even high-ranking Confederates expressed despair, at least in private. When Vice-President Alexander Stephens learned of the surrender of Fort Donelson, he told a friend: "The Confederacy is lost." Attorney-General Thomas Bragg lamented in diary entries during February that "dangers thicken around us. . . . Our people are disheartened. . . . Do what I will, I cannot drive the horrid picture from my mind."[13]

Jefferson Davis was inaugurated to his full six-year term as president on February 22 (until then he had been provisional president). He conceded in his inaugural address that "after a series of successes and victories, we have recently met with serious disasters." The inauguration took place during a driving rainstorm, which did nothing to lighten the mood. When someone asked Davis's coachman why the president and his footmen were dressed in black suits for the occasion, the servant replied wryly: "This, ma'am, is the way we always does in Richmond at funerals and sichlike."[14]

Far from the ferment of news and rumors in Richmond that magnified both victories and defeats, Southern whites elsewhere seemed equally depressed by the events of February and March. A plantation wife near Atlanta felt "very low spirited to night" because of "the gloomy state of the country." A North Carolina woman learned of the fall of Roanoke Island with "horror and dismay," while the news of Fort Donelson's capture was "sorrowful in the extreme. . . . I made an effort to throw off the gloom & talk of other things yet it all seemed hollow and artificial."[15] A planter in piedmont South Carolina had "no heart to comment on" the "bad, bad news! . . . Failure to our cause will bring us to such conditions, that I cannot dwell on it. God help us."[16]

The son of a wealthy Georgia planter, Charles Colcock Jones Jr. was an officer in an artillery battery defending the Georgia lowcountry. Although a graduate of the College of New Jersey in Princeton and of Dane Law School at Harvard, Jones despised Yankees and passionately embraced the Confederate cause. He agreed with his mother that "our recent disasters are appalling" because "the valley of the Mississippi is virtually almost lost, and our entire seacoast and Gulf coast with but few exceptions are completely in the power of the enemy." But he urged them not to "become despondent. . . . We are not conquered yet, nor will we be." A South Carolina captain likewise acknowledged to his wife that the enemy had gained a temporary advantage, "but this is no more than we have, all along, had of him, until lately. He did not succombe and give up for it — and shall we, who have so much more to fight for than he has, do so? I am completely surprised and mortified by the feeling manifested by our people." If we submit to the Yankees "we would be an humbled, down trodden, and disgraced, people." Never! "Our people [must] arouse themselves, shake off the lethargy . . . [and] meet the issue like *men*."[17]

The Confederate press picked up this theme, urging Southerners to forget the defeats and redouble their determination. "Let everyone . . . cultivate and promote a cheerful courage," proclaimed the pro-administration *Richmond Enquirer* on February 28. "Such as mope about, torturing themselves and vexing others with their unmanly repinings and cowardly fears" must be rebuked and shunned. "Despondency is but little better than treason." The *Richmond Dispatch* also filled its editorial columns with denunciations of "croakers" and "men in petticoats." The *Dispatch* agreed with the *Enquirer* that the whiplash stimulus of reversals would arouse Southerners to show "the people at the North" the true nature of Southern manhood. Then with renewed Confederate victories "their unfounded elation will give way to a dejection correspondingly profound."[18]

One Northern reader of such editorials (Southern and Northern newspapers were regularly exchanged or smuggled across the lines) claimed that they reminded him of "the boy who whistled through the grave yard to keep his courage up." The *New York Times* reprinted excerpts from several such Southern editorials under the heading "The Rebels Whistling to Keep Their Courage Up."[19] They would need to whistle even louder soon, for greater "disasters" to Confederate arms awaited them as spring came on.

After the loss of Fort Donelson and Nashville, the Confederate commander in that theater, General Albert Sidney Johnston, concentrated his remaining troops at Corinth in northern Mississippi. A key rail junction, Corinth became the next objective of Northern strategic planners. Halleck ordered Grant's and Buell's armies to unite at Pittsburg Landing on the Tennessee River, twenty miles north of Corinth, for an advance on the junction. But Johnston did not intend to wait for the Yankees to trap him. Instead, he called in reinforcements from the Gulf Coast to bring his army to 40,000 men at Corinth. Johnston planned to take the offensive against Grant's 33,000 before Buell's army arrived.

On April 6 the Confederates attacked at dawn near a church called Shiloh, which gave its name to the ensuing battle. They caught Grant by surprise and drove his army back toward the river. After a day of the most intense fighting this war had yet seen, with casualties on both sides totaling 15,000, Grant's beleaguered soldiers halted the Confederate onslaught at dusk. One of the Southern casualties was Johnston, who bled to death when a bullet severed an artery in his leg — the highest-ranking commander on either side to be killed in the war. General Pierre G. T. Beauregard, recently transferred from Virginia to the West, took command after Johnston's death. Believing that a continuation of the battle next morning would knock the Yankees into the river, Beauregard sent a telegram to Richmond that night: "After a severe battle of ten hours, thanks be to the Almighty, [we] gained a complete victory, driving the enemy from every position."[20]

The War Department in Richmond immediately released this telegram to the press, which trumpeted a great Confederate triumph. For several days Southerners believed they had reversed the war's momentum in the West. On the dismal, rainy night of April 6–7 at Pittsburg Landing, some of Grant's subordinates thought so too. They advised him to retreat to save what was left of his army. Grant replied: "Retreat? No. I propose to attack at daylight and whip them."[21] And so he did, reinforced overnight by a detached division of his own army plus three divisions of Buell's. By mid-afternoon the Confederates were in full retreat to Corinth after losing more than a quarter of their army. Beauregard never bothered to send a second telegram announcing these facts. And the heavy casualties suffered by the combined Union armies in the two days (13,000) plus reports that Grant was caught napping the first day dampened claims of Union victory. Nevertheless, the letdown in the Confederacy when Beauregard's boast of victory turned into a retreat added frustration to Southern disappointment.

That frustration possessed a sharper edge because of a simultaneous Confederate reverse on the Mississippi River. After the capture of Fort Donelson, Foote took his fleet of ironclad gunboats to the Mississippi for an attack on the heavily fortified Island No. 10 (so named because it was the tenth island downriver from the confluence of the Ohio and Mississippi). In cooperation with an army of 20,000 men under Union General John Pope, the river navy isolated the island and Pope's troops captured its 4,500 defenders and 109 guns on April 7 — the same day that Beauregard's battered army retreated from Shiloh.

This one–two punch produced a pair of headlines in an "Extra" edition of the *New York Times* on April 9: "Glorious News!" and "More Glorious News!" The capture of Island No. 10, declared the *Times* editorially, "must utterly discourage the rebels and show the futility of further resistance to the Government." Some rebels were indeed discouraged; a newspaper named the *Atlanta Confederacy* pronounced the Southern people to be "chilled, benumbed, and lifeless."[22]

The fall of Fort Macon in North Carolina and Fort Pulaski downriver from Savannah in April depressed Southern morale further. But all of these losses paled in comparison with the surrender at the end of April of New Orleans, the Confederacy's principal port and largest city.

Most Confederate troops in Louisiana had gone to Corinth for the campaign that culminated at Shiloh. The Confederate river navy on the lower Mississippi had steamed upriver to confront the Union fleet after the fall of Island No. 10. Left to defend New Orleans were a couple of half-completed ironclads, a few armed steamboats, three thousand militiamen, and two forts on the river seventy miles below the city. That was not enough to stop Union naval commander David Glasgow Farragut, a native of Tennessee who had remained loyal to the U.S. navy in which he had served for half a century.

Farragut headed the Gulf Expeditionary Force of twenty-four warships carrying 245 guns, nineteen mortar boats each containing a thirteen-inch mortar for high-angle fire against the forts, and 15,000 army troops. As matters turned out, the latter were not needed except as an occupation force. For a week in mid-April the mortars fired 17,000 shells at the forts without putting them out of action. Growing impatient, Farragut decided to steam past the gauntlet of enemy fire. Weighing anchor at 2:00 A.M. April 24, the fleet moved single-file upriver exchanging fire with the forts and the anchored ironclads, fending off fire-rafts and getting through with the loss of one ship sunk and three disabled. A Union officer described the battle as resembling "all the earthquakes in the world and all the thunder

and lightning storms together, in a space of two miles, all going off at once."[23] The fleet steamed up to New Orleans, where the hapless militia fled without firing a shot. The city surrendered with nine-inch naval guns leveled on its streets.

These events reverberated louder through both North and South than anything that had gone before. In Washington Elizabeth Blair Lee, whose brother was in Lincoln's Cabinet and whose husband commanded one of Farragut's ships, wrote that "our people are in a frenzy of exultation over New Orleans." The *New York Herald* predicted (yet again) that "we are within a month, or perhaps two weeks, of the end of the war," and gloated over "the great depression among the insurgents."[24]

The *Herald* scarcely exaggerated Southern gloom. From Richmond to New Orleans itself, newspapers lamented the "Great Disaster and Humiliation . . . sudden shock . . . unexpected and heavy blow . . . deplorable calamity . . . stunning blow . . . by far the most serious reverse of the war."[25] But in perhaps more examples of whistling past the graveyard, several editors claimed that there was "no cause to despond." The young American nation had lost all but two port cities in the Revolution, yet prevailed in the end. Southern armies in the vast interior of the country were still intact and full of fight. Confederate soldiers maintained their high morale, insisted the *Richmond Dispatch*. "No matter what disasters we may encounter, if this spirit continues to animate us, we must be successful in the end."[26]

This time, however, the spirits of some of the most resolute Confederate patriots remained drooping. "The recent disaster at New Orleans, & the probable consequences," wrote the fire breathing Virginia secessionist Edmund Ruffin, who proudly claimed to have fired the first shot at Fort Sumter, "have operated to depress my spirits more than all the previous losses to our arms & cause. I cannot help admitting . . . the *possibility* of the subjugation of the southern states." A North Carolina woman refused to believe the first report of New Orleans' surrender. When it was confirmed, "we came home deeply dejected, nay humiliated. . . . God help us we seem to be at the darkest now."[27] In her famous diary Mary Boykin Chesnut wrote simply: "New Orleans gone — and with it the Confederacy." Soldiers were not immune from such gloomy forebodings. A Virginia cavalry captain wrote to his wife that "our cause is hopeless unless some change takes place."[28]

Events during the next few weeks in the Mississippi Valley seemed to be frosting on the cake of Union victory. Farragut's fleet ascended the river to Vicksburg, compelling the surrender of Baton Rouge and Natchez along the way. On May 30 Beauregard evacuated Corinth before the combined Union armies, now commanded by Halleck, could surround and capture that rail junction's defenders. On June 6 the Union gunboats coming down the river annihilated the Confederate fleet trying to defend Memphis and forced the surrender of that city as well. The two Union fleets met at the last Confederate bastion on the whole of the Mississippi at Vicksburg, whose days seemed numbered. "We shall be disappointed if the National flag is not flying over every considerable city of the South by the 4th of July," exulted the *New York Tribune. Harper's Weekly* agreed that "the great work of suppressing the rebellion is in effect achieved."[29]

Two large and several small Confederate armies remained in existence, however, and they still controlled six-sevenths of the territory in the eleven Confederate states. Guerrilla operations behind Union lines and cavalry raids by such daring leaders as Nathan Bedford Forrest and John Hunt Morgan made Union jurisdiction in the other one-seventh precarious. Prospects would soon turn sour for Union forces in the Mississippi, Tennessee, and Cumberland valleys where they had so far enjoyed almost uninterrupted success. In the meantime, most eyes in both North and South focused on Virginia. If the blue tide could engulf the army defending Richmond and add the Confederate capital to its list of conquered cities, the rebellion might indeed be over by the Fourth of July.

In the Western theater the principal rivers thrust like an arrow deep into Confederate territory. In Virginia, by contrast, a half-dozen small rivers (navigable only below the fall line) lay athwart the line of operations between Washington and Richmond. They provided the Confederates with natural lines of defense. Once McClellan had recovered from his bout with typhoid fever in January 1862, Lincoln pressed him to move against the Confederate army standing defiantly in the Manassas Centreville area, only twenty miles from Washington. But McClellan insisted that the enemy forces commanded by Joseph E. Johnston outnumbered him (in fact, the Army of the Potomac had a two-to-one superiority in numbers). So he proposed to flank Johnston out of his defenses along Bull Run by transporting the Union army down the Chesapeake Bay to Urbana at the mouth of the Rappahannock River. With McClellan poised there only forty miles from Richmond,

Johnston would be forced to pull back to cover the Confederate capital.

Lincoln reluctantly consented to this plan — but only on condition that McClellan leave a sufficient force to defend Washington from a sudden rebel strike if the Confederates should decide to attack the Union capital instead of retreating to defend their own. Before McClellan could make his move, Johnston anticipated him by withdrawing from Centreville and pulling back to a position along the Rappahannock.

This withdrawal forced McClellan to revise his plan but not his basic strategy. Instead of landing at Urbana, he would transport his army of 100,000 or more men to Fortress Monroe at the tip of the Virginia peninsula formed by the York and James rivers. With a secure waterborne supply line protected by Union warships, he could then strike northwest toward Richmond sixty miles away. Lincoln again grudgingly approved, with the same stipulation about leaving behind a large enough force to defend Washington. The president, however, believed that the enemy *army* rather than Richmond should be McClellan's main objective; defeat the army and the city it defended could then be occupied. And to Lincoln it made more sense to fight the enemy near the Army of the Potomac's own base in Washington than to fight it near the enemy's base in Richmond. "Going down the Bay in search of a field, instead of fighting at or near Manassas," Lincoln told McClellan, was "only shifting and not surmounting a difficulty. . . . We would find the same enemy, and the same, or equal intrenchments, at either place."[30]

Secretary of War Edwin M. Stanton, who took office in January 1862 as a friend of McClellan but soon grew critical of the general's lack of aggressiveness. Stanton's ruthless efficiency and brusque personality earned him many enemies. (National Archives)

Lincoln's strategic grasp was sounder then McClellan's. But the president on this occasion deferred to the supposedly superior wisdom of his general — though Lincoln did relieve McClellan of his post as general in chief on the grounds that as commander of the Army of the Potomac in active operations he could not function in both capacities. This action may also have reflected Lincoln's reservations about McClellan, who first learned of it from a newspaper report. McClellan accepted his apparent demotion with good grace at the time, but his subsequent paranoia about "enemies" in Washington caused him to see it in retrospect as part of an intrigue "to secure the failure of the approaching campaign."[31] For the time being Commander-in-Chief Lincoln would function, in tandem with his new and ruthlessly efficient Secretary of War Edwin M. Stanton, as his own general in chief.

Stanton had taken the war office in January as a personal friend and supporter of McClellan. The general's slowness to move, however, his apparent reluctance to fight an enemy whose numbers he constantly exaggerated, and above all a dispute over the number of troops remaining to protect Washington began to turn Stanton against McClellan. The general left behind fewer troops than he had promised; some of them were raw recruits; and he counted as part of the capital's defenses the units that were operating a considerable distance away in the Shenandoah Valley. An angry Lincoln thereupon detached one large corps from McClellan's force, keeping it in the area around Fredericksburg where it could join McClellan as he neared Richmond or go to the defense of Washington, as circumstances dictated.

Lincoln and Stanton also heard ugly rumors that McClellan was really pro-Southern and had deliberately left the capital undefended. Neither believed this. They did not doubt McClellan's loyalty but they did begin to doubt his moral courage — his willingness to seize the initiative and fight. McClellan in turn began to believe that Stanton and Lincoln were withholding needed reinforcements because they had come under the sway of radical Republicans who wanted him to fail and to prolong the war until it became a war to destroy slavery. The poison of mutual suspicion seeped ever more deeply into the Army of the Potomac and the government it served.

Little of this infection was apparent to

the public as McClellan landed on the Peninsula and began his campaign in April. Instead of smashing through the thinly manned defenses at Yorktown, however, McClellan as usual overestimated enemy strength and settled down for a siege with what even he acknowledged was his superior weight of artillery. McClellan and his supporters in the Northern press (led by the *New York Herald*) were confident that, like George Washington and the Comte de Rochambeau four score years earlier, they would capture the enemy at Yorktown after a siege. "There can be no resistance offered by the rebels that can check the successful advance of this tremendous force," predicted the *Herald*.[32]

Johnston thought the same. When Confederate intelligence informed him that McClellan was about to open fire with his mortars and 100-pound Parrott rifles, Johnston pulled out on the night of May 3–4 and retreated toward Richmond. A sharp rear-guard action at the old colonial capital of Williamsburg on May 5 held off Union pursuit long enough for the rest of the army to get cleanly away.

McClellan considered his month-long siege to be a triumph at minimal cost in casualties. Lincoln was not convinced, for

Cheered by his soldiers, McClellan arrives on the Virginia Peninsula on April 5, 1862, to take command of the siege of Yorktown. (*Harper's Weekly*)

the rebels lived to fight another day. But as McClellan's ponderous advance brought the Army of the Potomac within six miles of Richmond by mid-May, Northern soldiers as well as civilians became cocky. Charles Harvey Brewster, a lieutenant in the 10th Massachusetts, was confident that "the rebels would have to give up pretty soon." A captain in the 71st Pennsylvania boasted that when the army attacked the Richmond defenses, "we will just go right over the works, for I do not think it possible to stay this enthusiastic army." A

Wisconsin soldier wrote home simply: "The next letter I send you will be mailed from Richmond."[33]

The evacuation of Yorktown forced Confederates to pull out of Norfolk as well, yielding the most important naval yard in the South to the Yankees. The captain of the CSS *Virginia* (popularly called the *Merrimac*), which had fought the USS *Monitor* to a draw in history's first battle between ironclad ships two months earlier, was forced to blow up his ship to prevent capture because she drew too much water to retreat up the James River. The James was now open all the way to a fort and obstructions at Drewry's Bluff only seven miles below Richmond. The capture of Norfolk "was second in importance only to that of New Orleans," declared the *New York Times*, which led the Northern cheerleading. "Jeff. Davis must fly from Richmond" and "the fate of the Merrimac . . . is a type of the fate of the rebellion, which also rushes to desperation and to suicide." It would not only be Davis who had to flee Richmond, declared the *New York Herald*. "We expect to announce before the end of the week . . . that Virginia is cleared of the ungodly rebel crew — government, army, editors, suckers, and leeches, camp followers and all."[34]

From Washington Elizabeth Blair Lee kept her husband, whose gunboat *Oneida* was helping clear the lower Mississippi of rebel resistance, informed of the mood in the Union capital. "It is believed in town," she wrote in April, "that Virginia will be evacuated without a fight." That did not prove to be true, but several weeks later she reported that "they have all fixed on Sunday next [June 8] for the taking of Richmond." In New York the wife of a municipal judge with connections to prominent Democrats including McClellan's political advisers, wrote in May, after the capture of Norfolk, that "now there may be truth in what Mrs. McClellan told us yesterday, that the war would be over by the Fourth of July."[35]

Those Southerners whom the *Richmond Enquirer* denounced as "alarmists" and "men of white lips, and blanched cheeks" thought so too.[36] Richmond seemed to be seized by panic during the second week of May. Members of the recently adjourned Congress rushed home with what Richmond newspapers branded unseemly haste. The secretary of war boxed up his Department's archives for shipment if necessary. The secretary of the treasury had

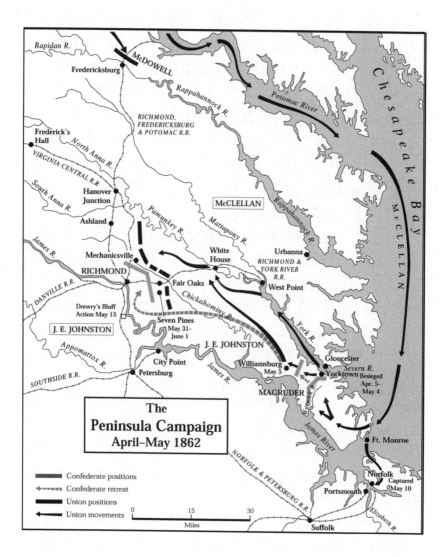

The Peninsula Campaign
April–May 1862

Confederate positions
Confederate retreat
Union positions
Union movements

0   15   30
Miles

the government's gold reserves readied for evacuation. Jefferson Davis sent his family to North Carolina, and Cabinet members followed suit. Wild rumors circulated that the whole government would decamp and Richmond would be abandoned to the enemy. Official denials by Davis and by Virginia's governor carried little weight. "No one, scarcely, supposes that Richmond will be defended," wrote War Department clerk John B. Jones on May 9. A young woman in Richmond said that she felt "like the prisoner of the Inquisition in Poe's story, cast into a dungeon with slowly contracting walls."[37]

Jefferson Davis felt the same. Observers commented on how "thin and haggard" and "greatly depressed in spirits" he appeared.[38] Visiting the president's household during these tense days was his niece, who wrote to her mother in Mississippi on May 7: "Oh, mother, Uncle Jeff. is miserable. . . . Our reverses distressed him so much. . . . Everybody looks distressed, and the cause of the Confederacy looks drooping and sinking. . . . I am ready to sink with despair."[39]

Davis's niece undoubtedly used the metaphor "sink with despair" unconsciously, but it was appropriate because the scuttling of the CSS *Virginia* was both cause and symbol of Southern despair. The *Virginia*'s spectacular one-day career of destruction back on March 8, when it sank the USS *Cumberland* and USS *Congress*, had been a source of Southern pride and

encouragement during an otherwise discouraging time. Although the arrival next
day of the USS *Monitor* had prevented further havoc by the Confederate ironclad,
the *Virginia* also prevented Union gunboats from going up the James River. Now
it existed no more. Confederate Ordnance
Chief Josiah Gorgas declared that "No one
event of the war, not even the disaster of
Ft. Donelson, created such a profound
sensation as the destruction of this noble
ship."[40]

The reaction was not confined to Richmond. In Georgia Lieutenant Charles C.
Jones Jr., who had kept a stiff upper lip
through previous reverses, believing they
would stimulate Southerners to fight
harder, finally succumbed to dejection
when he learned of the *Virginia*'s demise.
"Each event but proves more conclusively
than the former the power of our enemy,
his indomitable energy, consummate skill,
and successful effort," Jones wrote on May
12. "There is no denying that our country's fortunes are in a most desperate
plight, and . . . I see nothing ahead but
gathering gloom."[41]

These events on the battlefields and
rivers of America had important conse-

quences abroad. Like the secessionists of 1776, those of 1861 counted on foreign recognition and assistance to help them win their independence. The South's principal foreign-policy goals were European intervention to break the blockade and diplomatic recognition of the Confederacy as a nation.

The blockade was the chief issue during the war's first year. But on this matter, Confederate policy worked at cross purposes. Southerners fervently believed in the power of King Cotton to compel British and French intervention. The textile industry was the leading sector of the British economy and was important in France as well. Four-fifths of British and French cotton imports before the Civil War came from the American South. In 1861 the Union navy could not deploy enough warships to inderdict more than a fraction of Southern cotton exports. But a virtual embargo on such exports, enforced by committees of public safety and other forms of pressure in the South, kept almost all of the 1861 crop at home. The purpose was to persuade — really to coerce — the British to break the blockade in order to get cotton, thus provoking conflict and a possible war with the United States, which would ensure Confederate success.

This cotton embargo, however, created a catch-22 for Confederate foreign policy. Under international law as recognized by maritime powers at the time, a blockade had to be efficient to be lawful. In an effort to prove that the Union effort was a mere "paper blockade" and hence illegal, newly arrived Confederate envoy James Mason presented the British foreign office with long lists of ships that had gotten through the porous Union naval cordon in 1861. If that was the case, responded Foreign Secretary Lord John Russell pointedly, why was so little cotton reaching England? Mason could scarcely acknowledge the embargo, for the British would not take kindly to economic blackmail.

In any event, the King Cotton strategy was frustrated in 1861 by an economic fact: The bumper crops of 1859 and 1860 had actually produced a surplus of both raw cotton and finished cloth. Not until 1862 did this inventory disappear and the long-anticipated "cotton famine" begin to take hold. By then it was too late for Southern hopes of British intervention against the blockade. As a naval power, Britain traditionally depended on blockades in time of war. Her Majesty's govern-

James Mason of Virginia, author of the Fugitive Slave Act of 1850, who became the Confederate envoy to Britain during the Civil War and worked tirelessly for British recognition of the Confederacy. (National Archives)

ment was loath to create a precedent that might boomerang against Britain in a future conflict. On February 15, 1862, Lord Russell said that Britain considered the Union blockade legal so long as warships patrolled a port in strength "sufficient really to prevent access to it or to create an evident danger of entering or leaving it." The Union blockade certainly met this criterion by then.[42]

The principal Confederate diplomatic effort shifted in 1862 to the quest for official recognition. The South's model was French recognition of the fledgling United States in 1778, which had led step by step to active assistance that was crucial to American success. Both North and South

— one in fear and the other in hope — understood the importance of this matter. As early as May 21, 1861, Union Secretary of State William H. Seward had instructed the American minister to Britain, Charles Francis Adams, that if Britain extended diplomatic recognition to the Confederacy, "we from that hour, shall cease to be friends and become once more, as we have twice before been forced to be, enemies of Great Britain."[43]

Even if diplomatic recognition did not provoke a third Anglo–American war, Southerners expected it to be decisive in their favor. "Foreign recognition of our independence will go very far towards hastening its recognition by the government of the United States," declared the *Richmond Enquirer*, semi-official spokesman for the Confederate government. "Our independence once acknowledged, our adversaries must for very shame disgust themselves with the nonsense about 'Rebels,' 'Traitors,' &c" and "look upon our Independence . . . as *un fait accompli*." Confederate Secretary of State Judah P. Benjamin was confident that "our recognition would be the signal for the immediate organization of a large and influential party in the Northern States favorable to putting an end to the war." Moreover, "in our finances at home its effects would be magical, and its collateral advantages would be immeasurable."[44]

Benjamin's scenario was more than wishful thinking. Judging from the strenuous efforts by Union diplomats to prevent recognition and by the huge volume of news and editorial coverage of the issue in Northern newspapers, foreign recognition of the Confederacy would have been a grievous, perhaps a fatal blow. Recognition would have conferred international legitimacy on the Confederacy and produced great pressure for the United States to do the same. It would have boosted Southern morale and encouraged foreign investment in Confederate bonds. Recognition would also have enabled the Confederacy to negotiate military and commercial treaties with foreign powers.[45]

This question, however, also presented the South with something of a catch-22. Although Napoleon III of France wished to recognize the Confederacy from almost the beginning, he was unwilling to take this step except in tandem with Britain. (All other European powers except perhaps Russia would have followed a British and French lead.) British policy on recognition of a revolutionary or insurrectionary government was coldly pragmatic. Not until it had proved its capacity to sustain and defend its independence, almost beyond peradventure of doubt, would Britain risk recognition. The Confederate hope, of course, was for help in *gaining* that independence.

Most European observers and statesmen believed in 1861 that the Union cause was hopeless. In their view, the Lincoln administration could never reestablish control over 750,000 square miles of territory defended by a determined and courageous people. And there was plenty of sentimental sympathy for the Confederacy in Britain, for which the powerful *Times* of London was the foremost advocate. Many Englishmen professed to disdain the vulgar materialism of money-grubbing Yankees and to project a congenial image of the Southern gentry that conveniently ignored slavery. Nevertheless, the government of Prime Minister Viscount Palmerston was anything but sentimental. It required hard evidence of the Confederacy's ability to survive, in the form of military success, before offering diplomatic recognition. But it would also require Union military success to forestall that possibility. As Lord

Robert Cecil told a Northern acquaintance in 1861: "Well, there is one way to convert us all — Win the battles, and we shall come round at once."[46]

But in 1861 the Confederacy won most of the battles — the highly visible ones, at least, at Manassas, Wilson's Creek (Missouri), and Balls Bluff. And by early 1862 the cotton famine was beginning to hurt. Henry Adams, private secretary to his father in the American legation at London, wrote in January 1862 that only "one thing would save us and that is a decisive victory. Without that our fate here seems to me a mere matter of time." In February the *New York Tribune* acknowledged the critical foreign-policy stakes of the military campaigns then in progress: "If our armies now advancing shall generally be stopped or beaten back, France, England, and Spain will make haste to recognize Jeff's Confederacy as an independent power." Only Union victories — "prompt, signal, decisive — can alone prevent that foreign intervention on which all the hopes of the traitors are staked."[47]

The signal and decisive Union victories during the next four months fulfilled the *Tribune*'s hopes. In London, James Mason conceded that news of the fall of Forts

Charles Francis Adams, the skilled and experienced U.S. minister to Britain who worked tirelessly to prevent British recognition of the Confederacy. (*Harper's Weekly*)

Henry and Donelson "had an unfortunate effect on the minds of our friends here." Charles Francis Adams informed Seward in March that as a consequence of Northern success, "the pressure for interference here has disappeared." At the same time Henry Adams wrote to his brother in the army back home that "times have so decidedly changed since my last letter to you. . . . The talk of intervention, only two months ago so loud as to take a semi-official tone, is now out of the minds of everyone."[48] The London *Times* ate crow, admitting it had underestimated "the unexpected and astonishing resolution of the North." Even Napoleon's pro-Southern sentiments seemed to have cooled. From Paris the American minister,

William Dayton, wrote in April that "the change in condition of affairs at home has produced a change, if possible more striking abroad. There is little more said just now as to . . . the propriety of an early recognition of the south."[49]

News from America took almost two weeks to reach Europe. In mid-May Henry Adams returned to the legation from a springtime walk in London to find his father dancing across the floor and shouting, "We've got New Orleans." Indeed, added Henry, "the effect of the news here has been greater than anything yet." It must have been, to prompt such behavior by the grandson of John Adams and son of John Quincy Adams. While Adams was dancing, James Mason was writing dispiritedly to Jefferson Davis that "the fall of New Orleans will certainly exercise a depressing influence here for intervention."[50]

Mason did not stop trying, however. He urged Lord Russell to offer Britain's good offices to mediate an end to a war "ruinous alike to the parties engaged in it, and to the prosperity and welfare of Europe." Such an offer would be tantamount to recognizing Confederate independence. In a blunt reply, Russell pointed out that "the capture of New Orleans, the advance of the Federals to Corinth, to Memphis, and the banks of the Mississippi as far as Vicksburg" meant that "Her Majesty's Government are still determined to wait." Nevertheless, Mason worked his contacts among members of Parliament, who planned to introduce a motion in the House of Commons calling for recognition of the Confederacy. But Prime Minister Palmerston, in his singular style of spelling and capitalization, wrote in June that "this seems an odd moment to Chuse for acknowledging the Separate Independence of the South when all the Seaboard, and the principal internal Rivers are in the hands of the North. . . . We ought to know that their Separate Independence is a Truth and a Fact before we declare it to be so."[51]

Therefore, as Charles Francis Adams informed Seward, even among skeptics in Britain "the impression is growing stronger that all concerted resistance to us will before long be at an end." The danger of recognition, Adams had earlier noted, "will arise again only in the event of some decided reverse."[52] Indeed it would, and those reverses were soon to occur as the pendulum of battle swung toward the Confederacy in the summer of 1862.

Two

Taking Off the Kid Gloves
JUNE–JULY 1862

The first cloud on the horizon of Union military success in 1862 appeared in the Shenandoah Valley. A small Northern army had moved south into this fertile breadbasket of Virginia in conjunction with McClellan's advance against the main Confederate army defending Richmond. The Union commander was General Nathaniel P. Banks, one of the North's "political generals" appointed not because of his military skills but because of his political influence. It was Banks's misfortune that he faced Confederate General Thomas J. Jackson, known as "Stonewall" since his brigade's stand at Manassas the previous July. Jackson's mission was to create a diversion that would compel Lincoln to divert to the Valley some of the reinforcements slated for McClellan.

The bold, secretive, eccentric Jackson succeeded so brilliantly that he became the most renowned commander in the South and most feared in the North until his death a year later. From May 8 to June 9, 1862, Jackson demonstrated what could be accomplished by deception, daring, and mobility. With only 17,000 men he moved by marches so swift that his infantry earned the nickname "Jackson's foot cavalry." Using the terrain of mountains, valleys, and mountain gaps, Jackson pounced unexpectedly on separate enemy detachments that his forces always outnumbered at the point of attack, even though the total number of Union troops trying to combine against Jackson outnumbered him by more than two to one. Of the five battles that Jackson fought and won during this month, the main victory took place at Winchester on May 25 when the Confederates drove Banks's routed division in precipitate flight all the way across the Potomac into Maryland.

This battle caused a temporary panic in the North and elation in the South. It slowed the momentum of Union victory that had seemed irresistible. And the failure of converging forces to trap Jackson during the next two weeks produced great frustration in the North. Having predicted daily the imminent fall of Richmond, the Northern press was taken aback by Banks's "severe and most mortifying disaster" at Winchester, which created "astonishment and alarm" in the North. Nevertheless, declared the *New York Times* in perhaps a Northern version of whistling past the graveyard, Jackson's actions were but "an episode" that "will have no important result" and "cannot affect in the slightest degree the general progress of the campaign."[1]

To Southerners, Jackson's victories were much more than an episode. "The hearts of the people will thrill with joy," predicted the *Richmond Enquirer*.[2] And so they did. From Virginia to Louisiana, civilians and soldiers filled their diaries and letters with paeans of praise for "the tremendous whipping" that the "great and good" Stonewall had given Banks.[3] During the months of Confederate defeats, wrote a South Carolina woman who had three brothers in the army, "I poured out prayers to God for victory. . . . My prayer was heard. Stonewall Jackson gained a brilliant victory."[4]

While Jackson was escaping the mismanaged effort to trap him between two converging Union forces in the Shenandoah Valley, General Joseph Johnston launched an equally mismanaged Confederate attack on a portion of McClellan's army five miles east of Richmond on May 31–June 1. The most significant result of this drawn battle (called Seven Pines by the Confederates and Fair Oaks by the Federals) was the wounding of Johnston and his replacement by Robert E. Lee.

Lee's appointment elicited little enthusiasm in the South. His first field command in western Virginia had failed to dislodge Union forces from that region. Sent by Jefferson Davis in November 1861 to the South Atlantic coast, Lee had recognized that Union naval supremacy made defense of river estuaries impossible and had pulled Confederate defenses back to strategic inland points. Recalled to Richmond in March 1862, Lee became Davis's military adviser just in time to receive some of the blame for Confederate reverses during the spring. Some Southern newspapers nicknamed him "Granny Lee" or "Evacuating Lee." Few seemed aware that Lee deserved much of the credit for devising Jackson's Valley campaign. One of Lee's first actions as the new commander of what he designated the Army of

General Robert E. Lee, whose firm countenance only hints at the "audacity" that characterized his generalship. (Library of Congress)

Northern Virginia was to strengthen the earthwork fortifications ringing Richmond. This project produced another pejorative reference to Lee as the King of Spades. Critics failed to understand that Lee's purpose was to put the works in shape to be held by fewer men in order to release the rest for the counteroffensive he planned.

Many in the South, therefore, shared McClellan's opinion of Lee as "cautious & weak under grave responsibility . . . wanting in moral firmness when pressed by heavy responsibility . . . likely to be timid & irresolute in action." A psychiatrist could make much of this statement, for it really described McClellan himself. It could not have been more wrong as a description of Lee. A Confederate officer who knew Lee well said that "his name might be Audacity. He will take more chances, and take them quicker than any other general in history."[5] By this stage of the war, Lee had concluded that the Confederacy's best chance for victory lay in a spoiling offensive that would disrupt McClellan's methodical advance. Lee became the foremost examplar of an offensive–defensive strategy. He believed that the North's greater population and resources would assure Union success if it became a prolonged war of attrition. To forestall this prospect, Lee intended to gather the South's maximum strength and strike a blow to knock the enemy back on its heels.

Meanwhile, what was McClellan doing with his army of 100,000 men? Much of his energy went into a series of telegrams to the War Department complaining that he lacked this and that, the roads were too wet to move up his artillery, and he faced 200,000 enemy troops (the maximum number Lee would be able to bring against him was 90,000, the largest Confederate army ever assembled) and needed reinforcements before he could take the offensive.

While McClellan bickered with Washington, Lee acted. On June 12 he sent cavalry commanded by the dashing Jeb Stuart on a reconnaissance to locate McClellan's right flank. Stuart did the job; he then made himself famous and embarrassed McClellan's cavalry by riding all the way around the Army of the Potomac and returning to his own lines with the loss of only one man. Lee shifted most of his army north of the Chickahominy River and brought Jackson's troops from the Valley for an attack on the Union right scheduled for June 26. The previous day McClellan had probed Confederate lines south of the Chickahominy in an operation that, in retrospect, became known as the first of the Seven Days Battles. From June 26 on it was the Army of Northern Virginia that did the attacking — repeatedly, relentlessly, with a courage bordering on recklessness, without regard to heavy casualties that would total 20,000 Confederates (and 16,000 Federals) for the whole Seven Days.

McClellan went to pieces. He was

defeated, even if his army was not. After the largest battle of the Seven Days, at Gaines' Mill on June 27, he abandoned all thought of making a stand or launching a counterattack. When the Confederates assaulted the 30,000 Federals north of the Chickahominy at Gaines' Mill, McClellan had 70,000 men facing only 25,000 south of that river. But the distraught Union commander wired Washington on June 28 that he was under attack by superior numbers on *both* sides of the river. "I have lost this battle because my force was too small," he told Stanton. "The government must not and cannot hold me responsible for the result. . . . I have seen too many dead and wounded comrades to feel otherwise than that this Government has not sustained this army. . . . If I save this army now, I tell you plainly that I owe no thanks to you or any other persons in Washington. You have done your best to sacrifice this army."[6] A startled colonel in the telegraph office deleted the final two sentences before sending this dispatch to Stanton. The secretary and president did not see these accusations.

McClellan decided to retreat southward to a new base on the James River, where Union gunboats could protect his

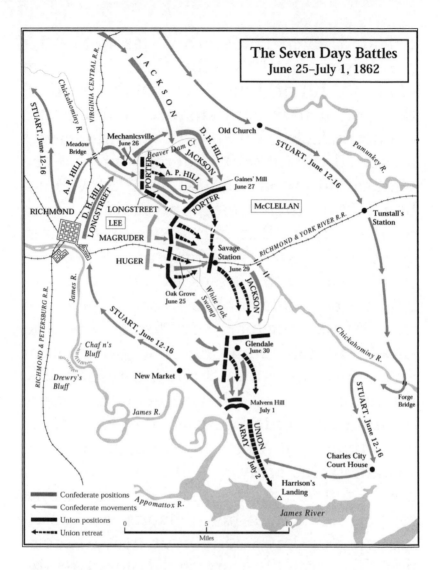

The Seven Days Battles
June 25–July 1, 1862

communications. The Army of the Potomac conducted a fighting retreat that punished the attackers, especially at Malvern Hill on July 1. Despite pleas from some of his subordinates that he use this battle as a springboard for a counterattack, McClellan continued the retreat. Confederates could justly claim a strategic victory in the Seven Days even though they won only one tactical battle (Gaines' Mill). On June 26 most of the Army of the Potomac was five miles from Richmond; on July 2 it was more than twenty miles away at Harrison's Landing on the James and its commander, still believing he was outnumbered by two to one, was in no mental shape to resume the offensive.

The Seven Days turned Southern despair to elation. "The almost funereal pall which has hung around our country since the fall of Fort Donelson, seems at last to be passing away," declared the *Richmond Enquirer* on July 4. "From out [of] the gloom and disaster of the past, the martial spirit has emerged" and "the superior skill and valor of our men over our brutal foe is incontestably established." Not to be outdone, the *Richmond Dispatch* proclaimed that "history has no record of such a succession of triumphs. . . . Throughout all time they will stand without parallel in the annals of warfare."[7]

From one end of the Confederacy to the other, sighs of relief turned into cries of rejoicing. "It is such good news that we can hardly believe it is true," wrote a young woman in Louisiana whose brother was with Lee's army. In Georgia, Lieutenant Charles C. Jones Jr. exulted that "the recent successes of our arms, by the blessing of God, have been even more remarkable and encouraging than were our former reverses depressing and unexpected." In Richmond itself the War Department clerk John Jones exulted that "Lee has turned the tide, and I shall not be surprised if we have a long career of successes."[8]

The Seven Days came as a huge shock to the North. Right up to the eve of the battles, the press had continued to predict the fall of Richmond by the Fourth of July. Instead, by that date the very fate of McClellan's army seemed in doubt. The plunge of Northern morale was all the greater because expectations built on almost uninterrupted success over the previous four months had been so high. A panic on Wall Street sent stocks as well as the value of the new greenback dollar into a temporary free fall. The *New York Times*, a good barometer of mainstream Northern opinion, acknowledged on July 3 that this "entirely unexpected" reverse "shatters the high hope which the whole country has of late indulged." Other newspapers found the situation "exceedingly discouraging and gloomy." They described the public mood as "disappointed and mortified" by this "stunning disaster" which had caused "misery" and "revulsion" throughout the North.[9]

Rather than celebrating Independence Day, "the nation is in the most eventful crisis of its history," declared the *New York World*. A nurse in an army hospital in Washington said the capital "was never so sad as today!"[10] An official in the State Department wrote that this Fourth of July was "the gloomiest since the birth of this republic. Never was the country so low, and after such sacrifices of blood, of time, and of money." A Connecticut congressman who talked with Lincoln reported the president to have said that when he learned of the retreat to Harrison's Landing, "I was as nearly inconsolable as I could be and live."[11]

Lincoln knew that in a democratic society whose citizen soldiers stayed in touch with their families and communities, morale on the homefront was as important as morale in the army. The roller coaster ride of public opinion in response to events on the battlefields, both in the North and South, was a crucial factor in the war. Victory pumped up civilian as well as army morale and sustained the will to keep fighting; defeat depressed morale and encouraged defeatism. The vigorous, free, and sometimes irresponsible press, especially in the North, intensified the volatility of public opinion by publishing frequent "Extras," by magnifying victories, and sometimes by initially minimizing defeats only to admit subsequently that a defeat was in fact a "disaster."

Americans were the world's preeminent newspaper-reading people, with by far the largest per capita circulation of any country. The war vastly increased their insatiable appetite for news and the impulsive response to it. "We must have something to eat, and the papers to read," said Dr. Oliver Wendell Holmes, whose son and namesake was a lieutenant in the 20th Massachusetts fighting in Virginia. "Everything else we can do without. . . . Only bread and the newspaper we must have."[12]

With time for reflection after the Seven Days, the astute "Lounger" columnist in *Harper's Weekly* (George W. Curtis) discussed the "lesson" of these battles: "Don't despise your enemy." Northerners had believed that the rebels were "demoralized, disheartened, and coerced; that their cause was hopeless, and the issue only a question of a little time," wrote Curtis. "We have all shared this happy confidence. . . . Let us be childish no longer." There was no reason for despair; the North could still win the war if its people made up their minds to work and fight harder. "There is not the least reason for doubt. . . . But there is every reason for keeping our eyes steadily open upon the facts."[13]

Several Northern newspapers picked up this theme. Like the Richmond press several months earlier, the *New York Times* and *Tribune* in particular tried to counter the "exaggerated depression" of public opinion with editorials titled "The Silver Lining" and "Counterblast to Croaking." A huge war rally took place in New York City on July 15, cheered on by the *Tribune* which insisted that "the dead speak to us with many thousand voices and point out the path of duty. The sacrifices already made . . . must not be in vain. . . . If the first flush of enthusiasm has passed away, it has been succeeded by a graver, sterner, more inflexible resolution."[14]

These cheer-up-and-fight-harder messages seemed to make little headway against the "sullen gloom . . . settling on every heart." The *Times* conceded that despite its efforts, "the great mass of the people are discouraged and disheartened."[15] The inventor of the telegraph, Samuel F. B. Morse, saw "no hope of Union. . . . I have no heart to write or do anything. Without a country: Without a country!" A member of the prominent Vail family of New Jersey, which had helped Morse develop the telegraph, thought matters were "darker than ever, just now. I have never felt any doubts about the result of this war until recently."[16]

The prominent New York lawyer and treasurer of the United States Sanitary Commission, George Templeton Strong, whose diary reflected the pulse of public opinion, reported through the heat of that summer of Northern discontent that "we have been and are in a depressed, dismal, asthenic state of anxiety and irritability . . . permeated by disgust, saturated with gloomy thinking. I find it hard to maintain my lively faith in the triumph of the nation and the law. . . . We begin to lose faith in Uncle Abe." Uncle Abe went through his own bouts with loss of faith. Lincoln's friend Orville Browning, senator from Illinois, saw the president on July 15. "He looked weary, care-worn, and troubled," reported Browning, who advised Lincoln to get some rest. "He held me by the hand, pressed it, and said in a very tender and touching tone — 'Browning I must die sometime.' "[17]

Perhaps inevitably, the setback of the Seven Days led to a round of scapegoat hunting. Northern newspapers accepted McClellan's estimate that he had confronted 200,000 enemy soldiers. The Democratic press took its cue from McClellan and blamed the administration for failing to send him the reinforcements he requested. By implication the fault was Lincoln's, but the Democrats concentrated their fire on Secretary of War Stanton (who had made no secret of his disillusionment with McClellan) and on radical Republicans whom they accused of deliberately sabotaging McClellan in order to get rid of him. Such men were "a faction of traitors," shouted the *New York Herald*, singling out editor Horace Geeeley of the rival *Tribune* as well as Stanton. The secretary of war was "the tool of the abolitionists, the organizer of disasters, the author of defeats." His "reckless mismanagement and criminal intrigues" produced the result that "thousands of lives have been thrown away, unnecessarily sacrificed, wantonly squandered, heedlessly murdered."[18] McClellan himself privately described Stanton as "the most depraved hypocrite & villain that I have had the bad fortune to meet with." If he "had lived in the time of the Saviour, Judas Iscariot would have remained a respected member of the fraternity of Apostles."[19]

The *Herald* was the most widely read newspaper in the Army of the Potomac at that time. Many officers and men echoed its opinions. McClellan remained their hero. For them as for him, it was an article of faith that they had not been outfought or outgeneraled, but beaten by superior numbers because traitors in Washington had withheld reinforcements. A soldier in the crack 83rd Pennsylvania, which had suffered 65 percent casualties in the Seven Days (including 111 killed), wrote on July 9 that "no one thinks of blaming McClellan. His men have the fullest confidence in his ability. . . . Anyone who saw how the rebels . . . pour five different lines of fresh troops against our one, can tell why he does not take Richmond." This soldier blasted Greeley and radical Republicans in Congress who used their influence with Lincoln "to prevent his being reinforced, to secure his defeat, and in some way to so prolong the war as to make the

Exhausted and discouraged Union soldiers stand down after the Seven Days Battles. (Library of Congress)

abolition of slavery a military necessity. Curses loud and deep are heaped on such men. Old Greeley would not live twenty-four hours if he should come here among the army."[20]

Many other soldiers echoed these sentiments, denouncing the "miserable fanatics who have been wishing" for McClellan's failure, while "his men almost worship him."[21] A New Jersey officer expressed unbounded bitterness toward "the *craven* politicians at home and in Congress, who will not give us reinforcements . . . men who to gratify personal feelings of envy, of hatred, of ambition and of the lowest self-ishness . . . keep an army on the offensive and at the same time see it outnumbered 2 to 1." As for Stanton, a Massachusetts officer considered him "the great murderer of his age, for to him are fairly imparted the deaths of all the men who have fallen since the siege of Yorktown."[22]

Greeley and most Republicans were much more muted in criticism of McClellan than his partisans were in criticism of them. An exception was Michigan's Senator Zachariah Chandler, who considered McClellan "an imbecile if not a traitor," and if a "traitor he ought to be shot." These statements, like McClellan's about Stanton, were made in letters to their wives. But publicly Chandler — and others — challenged the claim that the Army of the Potomac was outnumbered. In this they were right. McClellan's problem was not lack of reinforcements, they charged, but lack of the will to fight. "We feel much obliged to you for your exposure of that windbag and humbug McClellan," wrote one of Chandler's correspondents.[23]

Although McClellan's support within the Army of the Potomac was solid, it was not unanimous. Lieutenant Daniel

Brewster of the 10th Massachusetts, which had fought itself to exhaustion on the Peninsula, was "sick tired and disgusted" with McClellan's leadership. "This grand army we have bragged so much about, never made an attack on the enemy yet, he has always attacked us and surprised us, and generally worsted us." Brewster's own company "are all reduced to shadows and look as though they are on their last legs. They have a dreamy, listless look." Two of the army's best division commanders, Joseph Hooker and Philip Kearny, were privately scathing in criticism of McClellan. When Kearny received the order to resume the retreat after the repulse of Confederate assaults at Malvern Hill on July 1, he burst out: "We ought instead of retreating to follow up the enemy and take Richmond. . . . I say to you all, such an order can only be prompted by cowardice or treason."[24] One of the army's best regimental commanders, Colonel Francis Barlow of the 61st New York, pulled no punches in his private comments. "McClellan & many more of our Generals are damned miserable creatures," he wrote. "Unless there is a change in the leaders, the enemy will whip us again & again." The surgeon of the 5th Wisconsin agreed that "McClellan is a failure. . . . Never since the retreat from Moscow has there been so disgraceful a failure as the Peninsula campaign."[25]

Party politics in the conventional sense did not enter into these evaluations. Kearny, for example, was as opposed to radical Republicans and the kind of war they wanted to wage as McClellan was. But army politics in the sense of cliques and rivalries for promotion and preferment probably played a part. The army's senior corps commander, Erasmus D. Keyes, no friend of McClellan, deplored "the cloud of envy, jealousy, & malice under which this army has been shrouded."[26] The poison had seeped deeper into the Army of the Potomac. Only time would tell whether it would so weaken the army that "the enemy will whip us again and again," as Barlow feared.

During the weeks surrounding the Seven Days, Lincoln took several actions to revitalize the Union war effort. The impact of these actions in the short run was equivocal, though in the long run they changed the course of the war. On June 17 the president summoned General John Pope from the West to take command of the newly designated Army of Virginia, formed partly from the various units that had made such a poor showing against Stonewall Jackson in the Shenandoah Valley. Pope's task was to operate between Washington and Richmond and if possible to cooperate with McClellan in a pincers movement against the Confederate capital. Although he brought east a reputation as a successful commander, one of Pope's first actions confirmed the opinion of some fellow officers that he was a self-promoting braggart. "I come to you out of the West, where we have always seen the backs of our enemies," he declared in an "Address" to his new command shortly after the Seven Days. "I am sorry to find so much in vogue among you . . . certain phrases [like] . . . 'lines of retreat,' and 'bases of supplies.' . . . Let us study the probable lines of retreat of our opponents, and leave our own to take care of themselves. Let us look before and not behind. Success and glory are in the advance, disaster and shame lurk in the rear."[27]

No one, least of all McClellan, missed the point of this maladroit denigration of his army as well as of Pope's own army. And in Washington, Pope made no secret of his opinion of McClellan, whose

General John Pope, who did not endear himself to Union officers and soldiers in Virginia when he boasted of his successes in the Western theater. (National Archives)

"incompetency and indisposition to action were so great" that Pope said he could expect little cooperation from the Army of the Potomac. McClellan and his subordinates had a similarly negative attitude toward Pope. General Fitz-John Porter, commander of V Corps in the Army of the Potomac and McClellan's closest associate, declared after reading Pope's address that he "has now written himself down what the military world has long known, an ass." When McClellan learned in mid-July that Lee had sent Jackson with (initially) 12,000 men to confront Pope near the Rapidan River, McClellan wrote to his wife: "The Pope bubble is likely to be suddenly collapsed — Stonewall Jackson is after him, & the paltry young man [Pope was four years older than McClellan] who wanted to teach me the art of war will in less than a week either be in full retreat or badly whipped. He will begin to learn the value of 'entrenchments, lines of communication and of retreat, bases of supply etc.' "[28] Lincoln's hopes for concord between McClellan and Pope appeared doomed to disappointment.

The president also brought another general from the West to try to remedy problems in the East. Recognizing that his and Stanton's efforts to function as surrogate generals in chief had not worked very well, Lincoln called Henry W. Halleck to Washington and appointed him general in chief on July 11 — exactly four months after relieving McClellan from that post. McClellan considered the appointment of Halleck — "whom I know to be my inferior" — to be "a slap in the face."[29] McClellan may have been right on both counts. Halleck's high reputation owed more to Grant's success in the West than to his own. Lincoln expected his new general in chief to coordinate the strategies of all Union armies and to plan bold new offensives. But in this expectation he was also to be disappointed. Halleck turned out to be pedantic, fussy, unimaginative, and wary of responsibility.

These deficiencies would only gradually become clear to Lincoln. Meanwhile, he took other steps to beef up the war effort. Recruiting for Union armies had virtually ceased in April 1862. Some 650,000 men were then in the army — more than could be fully equipped and trained. Besides, it then seemed likely that the war would soon be over and won. By the end of June that notion had gone. The need was now imperative for more troops to cope with a rebellion that was more alive and well than anyone had thought. Yet Lincoln did not want to increase Northern alarm by issuing a new appeal for troops. So Seward met with Northern governors on June 30 and arranged to have them ask the president to issue a call for 300,000 new three-year volunteers so that "the recent successes of Federal arms may be followed up . . . to speedily crush the rebellion." Lincoln did so on July 1.[30]

Congress also passed a militia act on July 17 authorizing the president to call state militia into federal service for nine months (the previous limit had been three months) and to draft them if a state failed to fulfill its quota. By October 1862 these measures produced 421,000 new three-year volunteers and 88,000 nine-month militia. Most of the former and all of the latter were organized into new regiments rather than being fed into existing veteran regiments to bring them up to full strength. This practice was deplored by professional army men but preferred by state governors (who appointed the officers) and local communities that raised the companies for these regiments. Many of the new regiments eventually became first-class units that helped win the war. But some of those that went into action for the first time in Maryland and Kentucky in September and October 1862, with little training and no combat experience, may have been more hindrance than help to Union forces at Antietam and Perryville.

Confederate success in the Shenandoah Valley and the Seven Days Battles reopened the question of foreign recognition of the Confederacy. Many in Britain and France regarded these battles as confirmation of their belief that the North could never subdue the South. Many of the gentry and aristocracy in Britain tended to sympathize with the Confederacy, while the working class identified with the Union as the champion of free-labor democracy. But the cotton famine was beginning to hurt workers as hundreds of textile mills in Britain and France shut down or went on short time. Unemployment soared. Seward's earlier assurance that Union capture of New Orleans would lead to a resumption of cotton exports from that port was not fulfilled, as Confederates in the lower Mississippi Valley burned their cotton rather than see it fall into Yankee hands. Only a trickle of cotton made it across the Atlantic in 1862. The conviction grew in Britain and France that the only way to revive cotton imports and reopen the factories was to end the war. Pressure built throughout the summer for an offer by the British and French governments to mediate a settlement — which of course would mean Confederate independence.

As soon as news of Jackson's exploits in the Valley reached Europe (much magnified as it traveled), the government-controlled press in France and anti-American newspapers in Britain began beating the drums for intervention. The Paris *Constitutionnel* insisted in June that "mediation alone will succeed in putting an end to a war disastrous to the interests

Unemployed British textile workers queuing up for distribution of food and coal as the "cotton famine" took hold in the summer of 1862. (*Illustrated London News*)

of humanity." In similar language, the London *Times* said it was time to end this war that had become "a scandal to humanity."[31] The "humanity" they seemed most concerned about were textile manufacturers and their employees. The American minister to France, citing information coming to him from that country as well as from across the channel, reported "a strenuous effort . . . to induce England and France to intervene. . . . I should not attach much importance to these rumors, however well accredited they seem to be, were it not for the exceeding pressure which exists for want of cotton."[32] In mid-June the *Richmond Dispatch* headlined one story "Famine in England — Intervention Certain." Northern newspapers published many alarmist news stories and editorials about "British Intervention," "Foreign Intervention Again," and "The Intervention Panic" — all before news of the Seven Days reached Europe.[33]

Southerners hoped and Northerners feared that the Seven Days would greatly increase the chances of intervention. "We may [now] certainly count upon the recognition of our independence," wrote Edmund Ruffin. The *Richmond Dispatch* was equally certain that this "series of brilliant victories" would "settle the question" of recognition.[34] Under such headlines as "The Federal Disasters in Virginia — European Intervention the Probable Consequence," Northern newspapers regardless of party affiliation warned that "we stand at the grave and serious crisis of our history. The recent intimations from Europe look to speedy intervention in our affairs."[35]

Although perhaps not so critical as this rhetoric might suggest, the matter was indeed serious. "Let us hope that the North will listen at last to the voice of reason, and that it will accept mediation before Europe has recognized the Confederacy," declared the Paris *Constitutionnel*. On July 16 Napoleon III granted an interview to Confederate envoy John Slidell. The "accounts of the defeat of the Federal armies before Richmond," said the emperor, confirmed his opinion that the "re-establishment of the Union [is] impossible." Three days later Napoleon sent a telegram to his foreign minister, who was in London: "Demandez au government anglais s'il ne croit pas le moment venu reconnaître le Sud" ("Ask the English government if it does not believe the time has come to recognize the South").[36]

Les Anglais seemed willing — many of them, at least. The *Times* stated that if England could not "stop this effusion of blood by mediation, we ought to give our moral weight to our English kith and kin [Southern whites], who have gallantly striven so long for their liberties against a mongrel race of plunderers and oppressors." The breakup of the United States, said the *Times* in August, would be good "riddance of a nightmare." The *London Morning Post*, semi-official voice of the

Palmerston ministry, proclaimed bluntly in July that the Confederacy had "established its claim to be independent."[37]

Even pro-Union leaders in Britain and France sent dire warnings to their friends in the North. "The last news from your side has created regret among your friends and pleasure among your enemies," wrote John Bright to Senator Charles Sumner of Massachusetts on July 12. "I do not lose faith in your cause, but I wish I had less reason to feel anxious about you." Richard Cobden likewise sounded an alarm with Sumner: "There is an all but unanimous belief that you cannot subject the South to the Union. . . . Even they who are your partisans & advocates *cannot* see their way to any such issue."[38]

From France, Count Agénor-Etienne de Gasparin, who despite his title was a friend of the Union, wrote to Lincoln that only a resumption of Northern military victories could stem the tide toward European recognition. Lincoln took this opportunity to reply with a letter expressing his determination to stay the course. Yet, he added in a tone of frustration, "it seems unreasonable that a series of successes, extending through half-a-year, and clearing more than a hundred thousand square miles of country, should help us so little, while a single half-defeat should hurt us so much."[39]

Unreasonable it may have been, but it was a fact. A pro-Confederate member of Parliament introduced a motion calling for the government to cooperate with France in offering mediation. Scheduled for debate on July 18, this motion seemed certain to pass. The mood at the American legation was one of despairing resignation. The current was "rising every hour and running harder against us than at any time since the *Trent* affair," reported Henry Adams.[40]

But in a dramatic moment, Prime Minister Palmerston temporarily stemmed the current. Seventy-seven years old and a veteran of more than half a century in British politics, Palmerston seemed to doze through parts of the interminable debate on the mediation motion. Some time after midnight, however, he lumbered to his feet and in a crisp speech of a few minutes put an end to the debate and the motion (the sponsor withdrew it). Parliament should trust the Cabinet's judgment to act at the right time, said Palmerston. That time would arrive when the Confederacy's independence was "firmly and permanently established." One or two more Southern victories, he hinted, might do the job, but until then any premature action by Britain might risk rupture with the United States.[41]

This did not end the matter. James Mason wrote the following day that he still looked "speedily for intervention in *some form*." In Paris on July 25 John Slidell declared himself "more hopeful than I have been at any time since my arrival in Europe."[42] The weight of both the British and French press still leaned strongly toward recognition. And just before he left England in August for a tour of the continent with Queen Victoria, Foreign Secretary Russell arranged with Palmerston for a Cabinet meeting when he returned in October to discuss mediation and recognition.

Next to events on the battlefield and the worsening cotton famine, the slavery issue influenced European attitudes. Something of a paradox existed on this question, however. The American cotton wanted by British and French mills was nearly all grown by slaves. Yet most Europeans were antislavery. Britain had abolished slavery in its New World colonies in 1833 and France had done the same in 1848. The

British were proud of their navy's role as the world's police against the African slave trade. Many in Britain who were inclined to sympathize with the Confederacy found slavery a large stumbling block. If they thought at all about where the cotton would come from without slavery, they assumed that free black farmers would grow it.

In any event, Confederate envoys in Britain acknowledged early in the war that "the public mind here is entirely opposed to the Government of the Confederate States of America on the question of slavery." Lincoln recognized the importance of this issue. In January 1862 he reportedly said in a private conversation: "I cannot imagine that any European power would dare to recognize and aid the Southern Confederacy if it became clear that the Confederacy stands for slavery and the Union for freedom."[43]

When Lincoln said this, however, the Union did not stand for freedom — though a growing number of Republicans were calling for a war against slavery. Not understanding the crosscutting pressures from various quarters for and against emancipation as a Union war policy, and not appreciating Lincoln's need to keep border slave states and Northern Democrats in his war coalition, many European observers assumed that he could announce emancipation whenever he wanted to. Since "the North does not proclaim abolition and never pretended to fight for anti-slavery," asked Englishmen who might otherwise be inclined to support the Union, "how can we be fairly called upon to sympathize so warmly with the Federal cause? . . . If they would ensure for their struggle the sympathies of Englishmen, they must abolish slavery."[44] When a pro-Union MP said in the July 18 parliamentary debate on mediation that the American war was one between freedom and slavery, he was met with jeers and loud cries of "No, No!"[45]

Foreign-policy considerations were only part of the pressures pushing Lincoln toward a commitment to emancipation in 1862. "I am naturally anti-slavery," Lincoln insisted. "If slavery is not wrong, nothing is wrong." Yet, "I have never understood that the Presidency conferred upon me an unrestricted right to act officially upon this judgment and feeling."[46] Because he had no constitutional power to interfere with slavery in the states, and

112

because he needed to retain the support of border states and Democrats, Lincoln in the first year of the war repeatedly defined his policy as *restoration* of the Union — which of course meant a Union with slavery.

From the beginning, however, abolitionists and radical Republicans echoed the words of black leader Frederick Douglass: "To fight against slaveholders, without fighting against slavery, is but a half-hearted business. . . . War for the destruction of liberty must be met with war for the destruction of slavery." More and more Republicans — eventually including Lincoln — came to agree with this idea as the war ground on. They took note of Southern boasts that slavery was "a tower of strength to the Confederacy" because slaves did most of the labor in the South, thus enabling Confederates "to place in the field a force so much larger in proportion to her [white] population than the North." Douglass declared that he could not understand "why? Oh! why, in the name of all that is national, does our Government allow its enemies this powerful advantage? . . . The very stomach of the rebellion is the negro in the condition of a slave. Arrest that hoe in the hands of the negro, and you smite rebellion in the very seat of its life."[47]

Slave labor was so important in Confederate armies as well as on the home front that the government impressed slaves into service before it began drafting white men as soldiers. Thousands of slaves worked as army laborers, teamsters, cooks, musicians, servants, and in other support capacities. They provided much of the logistical "tail" of these armies (functions initially performed by white soldiers and civilians in Union armies) and thereby freed a high proportion of Confederate soldiers for combat duty. As time passed, more and more Yankees began asking: Why not convert this Southern asset of black labor into a Northern asset by confiscating slaves as enemy property, freeing them, and putting them to work for the Union?

The slaves themselves entered this debate in dramatic fashion. Many of them saw the war as a potential war for freedom as soon as abolitionists did. They voted with their feet for freedom by escaping from their masters to Union military camps in the South. By creating a situation in which Union officers would either have to return them to slavery or acknowledge their freedom, escaping slaves took the first steps toward achieving freedom for themselves and making the conflict a war for freedom as well as for the Union. They turned the idea of confiscation into a reality.

The issue came up early in the war at Fortress Monroe in Virginia, near the mouth of the James River. The only place in a Confederate state controlled by Union forces in early May 1861, the fort attracted runaway slaves from nearby Confederate camps. The Union commander at the fort was Benjamin Butler, who proved to be a better lawyer and politician than fighting soldier. Butler refused to return the escapees to their masters and ingeniously labeled them "contraband of war" subject to confiscation because they had worked for the Confederacy. The phrase caught on quickly; for the rest of the war slaves who came within Union lines were known as contrabands.

On August 6, 1861, Congress took a big step toward legitimizing this concept by passing a confiscation act that authorized the seizure of all property, including slaves, that had been used in aid of rebellion. Nearly all Republicans in Congress voted for this bill and almost all Democrats and border-state Unionists voted against it.

Frederick Douglass, who pressed Lincoln in 1862 to turn the war for Union into a war for freedom. (National Archives)

Thus began a process whereby the emancipation issue defined the sharpest difference between parties.

Many Union generals, like McClellan, were Democrats. Some of them, especially in border states where slave-owners professed to be Unionists, refused to admit fugitive slaves to their lines or returned them to their owners. But many soldiers and junior officers had other ideas. "I never will be instrumental in returning a slave to his master in any way shape or manner," vowed Lieutenant Charles Brewster of the 10th Massachusetts in March 1862. A soldier in the 8th Michigan described what happened when a "slave-hunter" came into their camp near

Annapolis to reclaim his property. The soldiers "pounced on him," and if he had not quickly decided that discretion was the better part of valor, "he would have lost his life in this Negro Hunt. As it was he got well frightened, & I presume will think twice before he goes into a camp of Northern Soldiers to reclaim biped property."[48]

Not many Union soldiers were principled abolitionists, but a growing number of them were becoming pragmatic emancipationists. "I don't care a damn for the darkies," wrote an Illinois lieutenant in April 1862, but "I couldn't help send a runaway nigger back. . . . I honestly believe that this army [in Tennessee] has taken 500 niggers away with them." In fact, "I have 11 negroes in my company now. They do every particle of the dirty work." An Illinois sergeant wrote from Corinth, Mississippi, that "every regt has nigger teamsters and cooks which puts that many more men back in the ranks. . . . It will make a difference in the regt of not less than 75 men that will carry guns that did not before we got niggers."[49]

Combining such practical considerations with their own antislavery convictions, the Republican majority in Congress enacted a

"Contrabands" coming into Union lines in Virginia. (Library of Congress)

new article of war on March 13, 1862, forbidding army officers to return escaped slaves to their masters — even those masters who claimed to be loyal Unionists. Having built up a head of steam, Republicans pressed ahead: from April to July they enacted and Lincoln signed legislation to abolish slavery in the District of Columbia, to prohibit it in the territories, and to confiscate the slaves of Confederate owners. "I trust I am not dreaming," wrote Frederick Douglass, "but the events taking place seem like a dream." A free black man in

Washington joyfully informed slave friends of the abolition of slavery in the District of Columbia. One of them "left the room sobbing for joy"; another "clapped her hands and shouted 'let me go and tell my husband that Jesus has done all things well.' . . . Were I a drinker I would get on a Jolly spree today but as a Christian I can but kneel in prayer and bless God."[50]

In March 1862 Lincoln had made a bid to seize the initiative on the slavery issue. He sent a special message to Congress urging passage of a joint resolution offering "pecuniary aid" to "any state which may adopt gradual abolishment of slavery." Congress complied. This offer was aimed at the border states, with the idea that their commitment to emancipation would deprive the Confederacy of any hope for their eventual alliance and thereby shorten the war. In a thinly veiled warning, the president told border-state slaveholders that if they refused this offer and the war continued, "it is impossible to foresee all the incidents which may attend and all the ruin which may follow."[51]

At a meeting with Lincoln on March 10, however, border-state congressmen questioned the constitutionality of the proposal, bristled at Lincoln's warning, and deplored the anticipated race problem that would emerge with a large free black population. Two months later Lincoln again appealed to border-state slaveholders. The changes produced by his proposal for compensated, gradual abolition "would come gently as the dews of heaven, not rending or wrecking anything. Will you not embrace it?" the president pleaded. But he then added ominously: "You can not, if you would, be blind to the signs of the times."[52]

Border-state representatives, however, seemed blind to the changes that appeared on the horizon in the summer of 1862. Jackson's and Lee's counteroffensives in Virginia and Forrest's and Morgan's raids in Tennessee and Kentucky put an end to prospects of imminent Northern victory. An important consequence of this reversal of momentum was to convince many in the North that they must "take off the gloves" (a metaphor that became a cliché) and fight harder. "The star of the Confederacy appears to be rising," wrote an Ohio colonel who came up with his own metaphors, "and I doubt not it will continue to ascend until the rose-water policy now pursued by the Northern army is superseded by one more determined and vigorous." It was time to stop conciliating Southern civilians, many of whom were thought to be "bushwhackers" who raided behind Union lines, fired at Northern soldiers from their houses, and harassed Union operations in any way they could. Senator John Sherman wrote to his brother, General William T. Sherman, of a growing sentiment "that we must treat these Rebels as bitter enemies to be subdued — conquered — by confiscation — by the employment of their slaves — by terror — energy — audacity — rather than by conciliation."[53]

Many Union soldiers on the front lines in the South were the first to espouse this notion of "hard war." "The iron gauntlet must be used more than the silken glove to crush this serpent," wrote an Illinois officer in June 1862. Charles Brewster of the 10th Massachusetts complained of McClellan's conciliatory policy toward civilians on the Virginia Peninsula. "The whole aim [in] this kid glove war," he wrote, "seems to be to hurt as few of our enemies and as little as possible." In August 1862 an Iowa private growled that "we have been . . . playing with *Traitors* long enough. We have guarded their property long enough, now is the time for action."[54] When Henry W. Halleck became general in chief, one of his first orders to Grant, now commander of occupation forces in western Tennessee and northern Mississippi, was to "take up all active [rebel] sympathizers, and either hold them as prisoners or put them beyond our lines. Handle that class without gloves, and take their property for public use. . . . It is time that they should begin to feel the presence of the war."[55]

Take their property. The principal form of property in the South was the slaves. A Wisconsin major insisted that "the only way to put down this rebellion is to hurt the instigators and abettors of it. Slavery must be cleaned out." The colonel of the 5th Minnesota, stationed in northern Alabama, wrote that "I am doing quite a business in the confiscation of slave property. . . . Crippling the institution of slavery is . . . striking a blow at the heart of the rebellion."[56]

Although many soldiers and officers remained opposed to fighting this kind of war, one prominent convert to the doctrine of hard war was General John Pope. In July he issued a series of general orders to his new command, the Army of Virginia, authorizing his officers to seize enemy property without compensation, to shoot captured guerrillas not in uniform who had fired on Union troops, to expel from occupied territory any civilians who refused to take an oath of allegiance, and to treat them as spies if they returned.[57]

This was just the ticket, declared the *New York Times*, which often represented the views of moderate Republicans — including the president. "The country is weary of trifling," according to the *Times*. "We have been afraid of wounding rebel feelings, afraid of injuring rebel property, afraid of . . . freeing rebel slaves. Some of our Generals have fought the rebels — if fighting it be called — with their kid gloves on" — a thinly veiled allusion to McClellan. But now "there is a sign of hope and cheer in the more warlike policy which has been inaugurated."[58]

Confederate spokesmen expressed outrage at Pope's orders; Robert E. Lee declared that this "miscreant Pope" must be "suppressed." But Southerners scarcely denounced Pope in stronger terms than did General McClellan. If the Union government "adopts those radical and inhuman views," McClellan wrote to his wife, "I cannot well in conscience serve the Govt any longer."[59] When Lincoln came to

Harrison's Landing on July 8 to see for himself the condition of the Army of the Potomac after the Seven Days, McClellan handed the president an unsolicited letter of advice on the proper conduct of the war. "It should not be a war looking to the subjugation of the [Southern] people," the general instructed Lincoln. "Neither confiscation of property . . . [n]or forcible abolition of slavery should be contemplated for a moment. Military power should not be allowed to interfere with the relations of servitude. . . . A declaration of radical views, especially upon slavery, will rapidly disintegrate our present Armies."[60]

Whether such a declaration would have disintegrated Union armies is doubtful. But McClellan did represent the views of his staff and several of his corps and division commanders, especially Fitz-John Porter. That general had written privately several weeks earlier that the army needed "to win the respect of the people" of the South if the Union was ever to be restored, "and by a conservative course to cause our enemies in the rear (the abolitionists) to be looked upon with contempt." One of the corps commanders not part of McClellan's coterie, General Erasmus Keyes, complained that McClellan's "favorites" had in

Keyes's hearing "cursed Congress, damned the Republicans and been of that type of Breckinridge Democrat who don't seem able to imagine we are at war."[61]

Lincoln was aware of these sentiments among prominent officers in the Army of the Potomac. On July 8 he read McClellan's letter of advice in the general's presence without comment. But the president's thoughts can be guessed. Several months earlier he might have agreed with much of what McClellan wrote. In his annual message to Congress the previous December, Lincoln had expressed a hope that the war would not "degenerate into a violent and remorseless revolutionary struggle."[62] But since then the war had become remorseless, and Lincoln was about to embrace the revolution. Democrats and border-state Unionists who complained about this turn toward what the *New York Times* was calling "an active and vigorous war policy" now elicited exasperation from the president. The demand of Southern Unionists "that the government shall not strike its open enemies, lest they be struck by accident," wrote Lincoln, had become "the paralysis — the dead palsy — of the government in this whole struggle." The war could no longer be fought "with elder-stalk squirts, charged with rose water," Lincoln said sarcastically. "This government cannot much longer play a game in which it stakes all, and its enemies stake nothing. Those enemies must understand that they cannot experiment for ten years trying to destroy the government, and if they fail still come back into the Union unhurt."[63]

In this mood Lincoln called border-state congressmen to the White House on July 12 to give them one last chance to accept his offer of compensated emancipation. The "signs of the times" about which he had warned them two months earlier were even more obvious now. "You can form no conception of the change of opinion here as to the Negro question," Senator John Sherman wrote to his brother the general. "I am prepared for one to meet the broad issue of universal emancipation." A conservative Boston newspaper conceded that "the great phenomenon of the year is the terrible intensity which this [emancipation] resolution has acquired. A year ago men might have faltered at the thought of proceeding to this extremity, [but now] they are in great measure prepared for it."[64] Lincoln bluntly reminded the border-state representatives on July 12 of the

One of many wartime photographs by Mathew Brady's studio that made Abraham Lincoln one of the most readily recognized figures in the world. (Library of Congress)

"unprecedently stern facts of the case." The pressure for emancipation "is increasing," he said. If they did not make "a *decision* at once to emancipate *gradually* . . . the institution in your states will be extinguished by mere friction and abrasion." But once again a majority of the border-state men turned him down.[65]

Disappointed and frustrated, Lincoln evidently made up his mind that very evening to go ahead with a proclamation of emancipation, grounded in his war powers as commander in chief to seize enemy property (in this case, slaves) being used to wage war against the United States. The next day Lincoln shared a carriage with Secretary of State Seward and Secretary of the Navy Gideon Welles on their way to a funeral for an infant child of Secretary of War Stanton (who was then enduring a torrent of abuse from Democrats for failing to sustain McClellan). During the ride Lincoln informed the two Cabinet officials of his intention to issue an emancipation proclamation. As Welles later recounted the conversation, the president said that this matter had "occupied his mind and thoughts by day and night" for several weeks. He had concluded that emancipation was "a military necessity, absolutely essential to the preservation of the Union. . . . The slaves [are] undeniably an element of strength to those who [have] their service, and we must decide whether that element should be for us or against us." The border states, Lincoln now recognized, "would do nothing on their own," and perhaps it was unrealistic to have expected them to take the lead. Thus "the blow must fall first and foremost on [the rebels]. . . . We wanted the Army to strike more vigorous blows. The Administration must set an example, and strike at the heart of the rebellion."[66]

Nine days later Lincoln called the whole

Cabinet together to announce his decision. They expressed varying degrees of support, and only Postmaster-General Montgomery Blair dissented. A former Democrat from Maryland who had turned Republican, Blair protested that the Democrats would seize on the unpopularity of such a measure in the border states and the lower North to gain control of Congress (at least the House) in the fall elections. Seward said that he approved of the proclamation but not the timing of issuing it immediately, during this period of public discouragement with the military situation. Seward had another reason as well for counseling delay. After months of sneering at the North for not adopting emancipation, the unfriendly European press had recently — and perversely — responded to signs of growing emancipation pressures from Republicans with charges that their purpose was to foment a slave insurrection in the South. Thus for reasons of both domestic and foreign policy, Seward advised Lincoln to postpone issuing the proclamation "until you can give it to the country supported by military success." Otherwise the world might view it "as the last measure of an exhausted government, a cry for help . . . our last *shriek,* on the retreat."[67]

The wisdom of this suggestion "struck me with very great force," Lincoln said later.[68] So he put the proclamation away to wait for a military victory. It would prove to be a long, dismal wait.

Three

"The Federals Got a Very Complete Smashing"
August–September 1862

Little good news for the Union came out of the Western theaters to offset bad news in Virginia during July and August. Quite the contrary, in fact. The dizzying pace of Union conquests in the Mississippi Valley ended abruptly in June. Late that month the Union gunboat flotilla from upriver and part of Farragut's fleet from downriver met at Vicksburg. For the next month these two previously unbeatable task forces, supported by 3,000 army soldiers, tried in vain to batter into submission this "Gibraltar of the West," as Confederates labeled it. Situated on a 200-foot bluff and heavily fortified, Vicksburg could be invested by a land force only from the east. Not until 1863 would a Union commander figure out a way to do that. For several weeks in July 1862 the navy's two hundred guns and twenty-three mortars pounded Vicksburg and took heavy fire in return. The contest proved a standoff. Northern soldiers tried to dig a bypass canal out of range of Vicksburg's batteries, but low water in the Mississippi foiled their efforts. More than half of the soldiers and sailors fell sick with various maladies including typhoid, dysentery, and malaria, with several dying every day.

Farragut began to fear that his deep-draft ocean-going vessels would be trapped by the falling river, and prepared to pull out. Before he could leave, however, an intrepid Rebel sea dog gave the Yankees a black eye. The Confederates had been building an ironclad gunboat up the jungle-shrouded Yazoo River. Commanded by Lieutenant Isaac Newton Brown, a thirty-year antebellum veteran of the U.S. Navy, the CSS *Arkansas* steamed down the Yazoo to take on the whole Union fleet in mid-July. It burst like an apparition on the surprised Union vessels, tied up on either bank with steam down. The *Arkansas* fired its ten guns, as Brown later wrote, "to every point of the circumference, without the fear of hitting a friend or missing an enemy."[1] To Farragut's disgust, the

Arkansas ran the gauntlet of Union fire and tied up under the protection of Vicksburg's guns. The Southern press puffed the *Arkansas*'s exploits into a great victory, and so it appeared when the two Union fleets gave up and separately retreated upriver and down at the end of July.[2]

Union forces in Tennessee and northern Mississippi experienced even greater embarrassments. In part the Federals were victims of their own earlier success. After the capture of Corinth (May 30) and Memphis (June 6), the captors needed to divert several combat units to occupation duties in the forty thousand or more square miles they had conquered. Declining river levels in this unusually dry summer made them dependent on railroads for supply, so they had to divert even more troops to protect the rails and bridges from frequent guerrilla and cavalry raids. When Halleck went to Washington to become general in chief in July, Grant assumed command of these occupation forces. For the next three months he had his hands full dealing with guerrillas, contrabands, Northern merchants seeking trading permits, and efforts by two small Confederate armies to recapture Corinth.

Meanwhile Buell took his Army of the Ohio eastward to capture Chattanooga and accomplish Lincoln's cherished goal of liberating East Tennessee. He failed spectacularly. By late August Buell found himself compelled to abandon this campaign and race northward to prevent the loss of Kentucky as well as central Tennessee. Like McClellan, Buell was a political conservative who believed in a "soft" war to conciliate rather than to coerce Southern civilians back into the Union. He was therefore reluctant to deal harshly with guerrillas who cut his supply lines and harassed his movements with nightly attacks on bridges and outposts.

Worse was yet to come. In early July two of the Confederacy's ablest and boldest cavalry leaders rode forth on raids deep behind Union lines to wreak havoc and capture supply depots all over central Kentucky and Tennessee. On July 4 John Hunt Morgan left Knoxville with eight hundred troopers, Kentucky rebels to a man. They headed north into their native state where during the next twenty-four days they rode a thousand miles, destroyed several supply depots, captured and paroled twelve hundred prisoners at various Union posts, and returned home with the loss of fewer than ninety men.

Meanwhile Nathan Bedford Forrest rode out of Chattanooga on July 6 at the head of a thousand men. Bluffing the Union garrison of equal size at Murfreesboro into surrendering, Forrest tore up the railroad, captured a million dollars worth of supplies, and then burned three bridges on the line south of Nashville that Buell depended on for supplies. When Union crews finally repaired the damage, Morgan's merry men struck again, capturing a train and pushing the flaming boxcars into an 800-foot tunnel north of Nashville, causing the timbers to burn and the tunnel to collapse.

All of this was embarrassing enough and convinced Union commanders that to cope with enemy cavalry raids they must develop effective cavalry of their own — something that was a long time in coming. But the damage to the Union cause was more than psychological. The *Richmond Enquirer* may have exaggerated when it claimed that "Forrest in Tennessee and Morgan in Kentucky have done much to retrieve the disasters that lost us parts of both those States." But it did not exaggerate much. "Our cavalry is paving the way for me in Middle Tennessee and Ken-

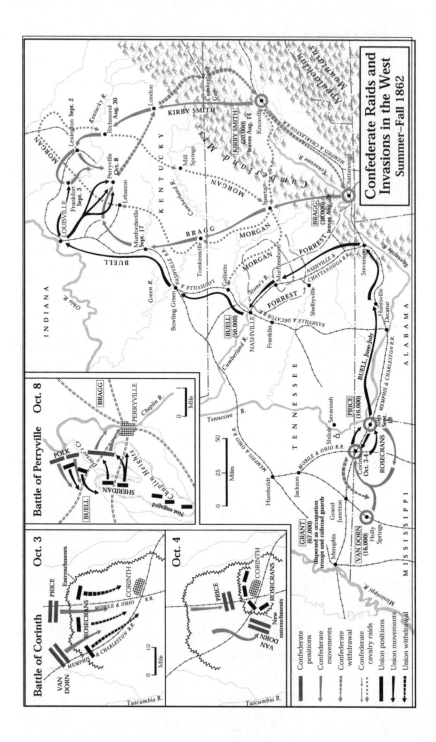

Confederate Raids and Invasions in the West
Summer-Fall 1862

Battle of Perryville   Oct. 8

Battle of Corinth   Oct. 3   Oct. 4

Confederate positions
Confederate movements
Confederate withdrawal
Confederate cavalry raids
Union positions
Union movements
Union withdrawal

136

tucky," wrote General Braxton Bragg in late July.[3]

Bragg had taken command of the Confederate Army of Tennessee after the evacuation of Corinth. As Buell crawled toward Chattanooga, Bragg moved some 35,000 troops toward that city, mostly by a round-about rail route, and got there well before Buell approached. In cooperation with General Edmund Kirby Smith, who commanded 18,000 Confederate soldiers in Knoxville, Bragg planned an offensive into central and eastern Kentucky. Smith started first, on August 14, and Bragg departed Chattanooga August 28. In tandem they moved north on parallel routes about a hundred miles apart. On August 30 Kirby Smith captured a Union garrison of 4,000 men (mostly new troops recruited that summer) at Richmond, Kentucky. Smith marched into Lexington and on to Frankfort, the state capital, where he prepared to install a Confederate governor of Kentucky.

Bragg's army advanced into middle Tennessee, forcing Buell to break off his own campaign against Chattanooga and rush northward to defend Nashville. Bragg bypassed the city and captured another garrison of 4,000 Union soldiers (also mostly new regiments) at Munfordville in Kentucky, only sixty miles south of Louisville. Panic seized Unionists in that city; even Cincinnati declared a state of emergency. Buell's Army of the Ohio continued north to its namesake river at Louisville, while thousands of contrabands along the 225 miles from which Buell had withdrawn found themselves in Confederate territory and in slavery again. On September 5 Bragg issued a congratulatory order to his troops: "COMRADES: . . . The Enemy is in full retreat, with consternation and demoralization devastating his ranks. . . . Alabamians! your State is redeemed. Tennesseans! . . . You return conquerors. Kentuckians! the first great blow has been struck for your freedom."[4]

In the Eastern states, most attention focused on events in Virginia and Maryland. When the New York press could spare a moment for the Western theater, the news seemed "gloomy in the extreme," for the campaign there "loses to the Union cause more than it gained in the brilliant campaign of last spring." But the danger to that cause appeared even more serious closer to home. From Washington on August 27 Lieutenant Charles Francis

Adams Jr., of the 1st Massachusetts Cavalry, wrote to his father in London: "The air of this city seems thick with treachery; our army seems in danger of utter demoralization and I have not since the war began felt such a tug on my nerves. . . . Everything is ripe for a terrible panic."[5]

How had matters come to such a pass? After the Seven Days the Army of the Potomac licked its wounds and tried to rest and refit at Harrison's Landing. But malaria, dysentery, and typhoid during this sickly season on the Virginia Peninsula subtracted more men from the ranks than were added by recovered wounded and returning stragglers. Send me reinforcements, McClellan asked the government, and I will resume the offensive even though Lee has 200,000 men. Lincoln's private response was very much to the point. On July 25 he told Senator Orville Browning that if by some miracle he could send 100,000 men to McClellan, the general would suddenly discover that Lee had 400,000.[6]

Lincoln's words were prescient. That same day the new General-in-Chief Henry W. Halleck visited McClellan to discuss what to do with his army. With 30,000 reinforcements, said McClellan, he could take Richmond. Only 20,000 were available, said Halleck. If that was not sufficient, the Army of the Potomac would have to be withdrawn from the Peninsula. Alarmed, McClellan agreed to 20,000. As soon as Halleck returned to Washington, however, a telegram from McClellan arrived asking for 50,000. That was the final straw. Halleck ordered McClellan to transfer his army to northern Virginia to reinforce Pope. McClellan had been hoisted by his own petard. If Lee really had 200,000 men holding a position between McClellan's 90,000 and Pope's 40,000, Halleck pointed out, the Confederates could use their interior lines to strike Pope and McClellan in turn with superior numbers. Thus it was imperative to combine the two Union armies to shield Washington.[7]

McClellan bitterly protested these orders, but Halleck, backed by Lincoln, insisted. Convinced that McClellan's inactive army posed little danger, Lee by early August had already shifted 24,000 troops under Jackson to confront Pope. Rumor magnified this force — Jackson's reputation was worth several divisions. This perceived threat to Pope convinced Lincoln of the need to transfer McClellan's army. On

August 9 near Culpeper, Jackson clashed with part of Pope's army — commanded by Jackson's old victim in the Valley, Nathaniel Banks — and defeated it in the battle of Cedar Mountain. McClellan learned of this outcome with satisfaction. In a letter to his wife, he predicted that Pope "will be badly thrashed within two days . . . very badly whipped he will be & ought to be — such a villain as he is ought to bring defeat upon any cause that employs him." Then "they will be very glad to turn over the redemption of their affairs to me. I won't undertake it unless I have full & entire control."[8]

These shocking words help explain why McClellan was in no hurry to obey orders to reinforce Pope. He received those orders on August 3; the first units did not leave until August 14; the last troops finally embarked at Fortress Monroe for Washington on September 3. As they left the Peninsula, the mood of many soldiers was sour and depressed. "We have fought more desperately, lost more men, and endured more hardships than any army under the sun, and all for nothing," wrote Charles Brewster of the 10th Massachusetts. As a New York regiment disembarked in Alexandria after transfer from the Peninsula, one of its officers felt "sorrowful and humiliated when looking back over a year and finding ourselves on the same ground as then. The debris of the Grand Army [has] come back to its starting place with its ranks decimated, its morale failing, while thousands who sleep their last sleep on the Peninsula demand the cause of their sacrifice."[9]

McClellan himself departed the Peninsula on August 23, uncertain whether he or Pope would command the combined armies. "I don't see how I can remain in the service if placed under Pope — it would be too great a disgrace," he wrote his wife. But if "Pope is beaten," which McClellan expected, "they may want me to save Washn again." Once they "suffer a terrible defeat" and Pope is "disposed of . . . I *know* that with God's help I can save them."[10]

Lee and Jackson were doing their best to see that Pope was "disposed of." In mid-August Lee left 22,000 men to defend Richmond and moved north with the rest to reinforce Jackson for an attack on Pope before McClellan's troops could join him. For ten days Lee's reunited force of 55,000 carried out a campaign of thrust and parry with Pope's army of equal size. Pope pulled back north of the Rappahannock River but skillfully avoided giving Lee an opportunity to attack. With the first of McClellan's divisions about to reach Pope in the last week of August, Lee decided on a typically bold but dangerous maneuver. He split his army and sent Jackson with half of it on a wide flanking movement around Pope's right and rear to sever his supply line.

Pope's scouts detected Jackson's march to the northwest on August 25 and reported that he was heading for his old haunts in the Shenandoah Valley. They failed to detect Jackson's turn eastward on the 26th. Jackson's foot cavalry logged fifty miles in their two-day march and swarmed like locusts on the huge Union supply depot at Manassas Junction twenty miles in Pope's rear. The famished rebels feasted on what they could eat and carry, and put the rest to the torch.

Pope had been outgeneralled, but he hoped to turn this embarrassment into an opportunity to "bag Jackson" before the other half of the Army of Northern Virginia could join him. But first he had to find Jackson. The slippery Stonewall had moved his three divisions over separate routes from Manassas Junction to a wooded ridge just west of the Bull Run battlefield of the previous year. Pope's overworked cavalry reported Jackson to be here, there, and everywhere. From Pope's headquarters on August 28 poured a series of confusing orders to his own army and to four divisions from the Army of the Potomac plus two from Burnside's army that had been transferred from North Carolina.

When and if united, these reinforcements would give Pope some 75,000 men (to Lee's 50,000 when united). But the Union divisions from three different armies had never fought together before, and rivalries and jealousies among some of their generals did not augur well. Commander of two of the Army of the Potomac divisions was McClellan's protégé Fitz-John Porter, who had called Pope an "Ass" a month earlier and had not changed his mind since. "Pope is a fool," Porter wrote privately, and the administration that had appointed him was no better. "Would that this army was in Washington to rid us of incumbents ruining our country."[11]

Just before sunset on August 28 one of Pope's divisions found Jackson. As this division marched unaware next to the Confederates hiding in the woods, Jackson could not resist the temptation to attack

Wreckage left by Stonewall Jackson's troops after they appropriated and destroyed Union supplies at Manassas Junction, Virginia, on August 27, 1862. (Library of Congress)

them. A vicious firefight continued until dark with neither side giving an inch. That night a new flurry of orders went out to Federal units, which began to concentrate in front of Jackson at dawn. Thinking that Jackson was retreating to join Longstreet (in reality Longstreet was advancing to join Jackson), Pope hurled his arriving divisions in piecemeal attacks against a strong Confederate position along the cuts and fills of an unfinished railroad. Pope managed to get only 32,000 of his men in action against Jackson's 22,000 on August 29.

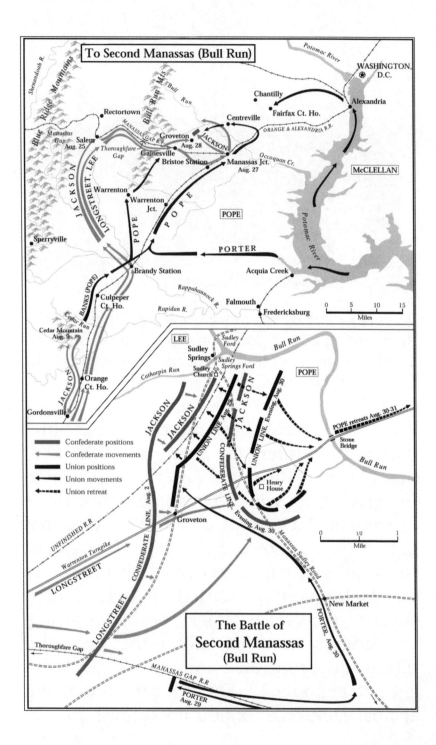

To Second Manassas (Bull Run)

The Battle of
Second Manassas
(Bull Run)

Confederate positions
Confederate movements
Union positions
Union movements
Union retreat

146

Porter's troops came up on the Union left in position to move against Jackson's flank, but having no orders and misled by a dust-cloud that Stuart's cavalry kicked up to convince him that a large body of the enemy was in front of him, Porter did nothing. Later in the day Pope ordered him to attack Jackson's right flank. By then Longstreet's corps had arrived and closed up on Jackson's flank, so Porter declined to obey the order. For this refusal he was, five months later, court-martialed and cashiered from the service. Long after the war Porter received a new trial, which reversed the verdict because of evidence of Longstreet's presence. Porter was, in part, the victim of the poisonous atmosphere in 1862–1863. But he had not concealed his opinions of Pope, of Republicans and abolitionists, and of Lincoln and Stanton. Moreover, his 10,000 veteran soldiers remained idle on August 29. Longstreet's presence notwithstanding, this idleness contributed to Pope's inability to dislodge Jackson.

On August 30 Lee pulled back some units to realign them for another flanking move around Pope. Again misinterpreting these movements as an enemy retreat, Pope remained unaware of Longstreet's presence and launched a full-scale attack on Jackson's half of the Army of Northern Virginia. When they were fully engaged, Longstreet counterattacked against Pope's virtually open left flank. "The slaughter was very heavy," wrote the twenty-four-year-old Major Walter Taylor, Lee's adjutant who was all over the battlefield carrying orders from the commander. "On some parts of the field their dead lie in files."[12] Through the long August afternoon the Federals fell back to Henry House Hill, where the heaviest fighting had taken place thirteen months earlier. Here a desperate twilight stand finally halted the Confederates. During the night a dispirited Union army retreated across Bull Run. Instead of following directly, Lee sent Jackson's tired, hungry men on another flanking march around Pope's right. During a torrential downpour on September 1, two Union divisions stopped them at Chantilly, only fifteen miles from Washington.

This second battle of Bull Run was a defeat fully as humiliating as the first, with greater potential danger to the Union cause. Angry recriminations flew in all directions. Most of the men in Pope's Army of Virginia as well as the Army of the

Potomac units that had fought there were demoralized, disgusted, and bitter toward Pope, whom they blamed for blunders and mismanagement. Pope in turn blamed Porter and McClellan.

Indeed, McClellan had much to answer for. He was at Alexandria with two corps of the Army of the Potomac during the battle. On August 27 and 28 Halleck repeatedly ordered him to send William B. Franklin's corps to Pope, to be followed by Edwin V. Sumner's corps. Back from McClellan came as many telegrams explaining why "neither Franklin's nor Sumner's corps is now in condition to move and fight a battle" — because their artillery and cavalry had not arrived. Pope did not need cavalry and could get along without artillery, said Halleck; he needed the infantry of these veteran corps. "There must be no further delay in moving Franklin's corps toward Manassas," Halleck wired McClellan on the evening of August 28. McClellan replied that Franklin would march in the morning. But next day he halted Franklin six miles out, in direct disobedience to Halleck's orders. The general in chief, exhausted from sleepless nights dealing not only with this crisis but also with the simultaneous Confederate invasion of Kentucky, could not budge McClellan. Franklin's corps stayed where it was and its 10,000 men went into camp within sound of the battle.[13]

Franklin was another of McClellan's protégés, and his soldiers took their cue from him. When Pope's discouraged survivors retreated wearily toward Washington on the night of August 30, they encountered the advance units of Franklin's corps, which had made it as far as Centreville that day. "Some of the more frank among them," wrote one of Pope's men, "expressed their delight at the defeat of Pope and his army. . . . Disgusted and sick at heart, we continued our slow march along." General Carl Schurz, one of Pope's division commanders, overheard some of Franklin's subordinates voice "their pleasure at Pope's discomfiture without the slightest concealment, and [they] spoke of our government in Washington with an affectation of supercilious contempt."[14]

In a telegram to Lincoln on August 29, McClellan revealed his real reason for halting Franklin and not hurrying up Sumner. The best course, suggested McClellan, might be "to leave Pope to get out of his scrape & at once use all our means to make the Capitol perfectly safe."

The president was appalled. McClellan "wanted Pope defeated," Lincoln told his private secretary. All evidence indicates that Lincoln was right. General Sumner "broke out in hot anger when he learned that McClellan had said his corps was not in a condition for fighting," according to Lincoln's secretary. "If I had been ordered to advance right on," Sumner later testified, "I should have been in that Second Bull Run battle with my whole force."[15]

These were dark, dismal days in the North — perhaps the darkest of many such days during the war. "For the first time," wrote the Washington bureau chief of the *New York Tribune* on September 1, "I believe it possible . . . that Washington may be taken."[16] With remarkable unanimity, newspapers of various political persuasions agreed that "the Country is in . . . extreme peril. The Rebels seem to be pushing forward their forces all along the border line from the Atlantic to the Missouri." And, "disguise it as we may, the Union arms have been repeatedly, disgracefully, and decisively beaten." Unless there was some change, "the Union cause is doomed to a speedy and disastrous overthrow."[17]

"Despondency was seen everywhere" on the streets of New York, according to many observers. Among Unionists in Baltimore "the mortification is great and the disappointment so deep that every man seems to carry his feelings in his countenance."[18] George Templeton Strong described September 3 as "a day of depressing malignant dyspepsia. . . . We the people have been in a state of nausea and irritation all day long." Four days later Strong believed that "the North is rapidly sinking just now, as it has been sinking rapidly for two months and more." The *New York Times* reported that many people were asking: "*Of what use* are all these terrible sacrifices? Shall we have nothing but defeat to show for all our valor?"[19]

Demoralization on the Northern home front was bad enough. Demoralization in the army was at least as bad — and potentially more deadly. A New Hampshire captain whose regiment had lost heavily at Bull Run declared that "the whole army is disgusted. . . . You need not be surprised if success falls to the rebels with astonishing rapidity." "Our men are sick of the war," wrote Washington Roebling, a New Jersey officer and future builder of the Brooklyn Bridge. "They fight without an aim and without enthusiasm; they have no confidence in their leaders." A New York colonel thought "there is no prospect or hopes of success in this war."[20] A brigade commander who had fought at both Bull Run and Chantilly wrote to his wife on September 4: "I believe that the war is nearly over, for the enemy is an audacious one. . . . I am more despondent than ever before." Another brigade commander confirmed that "there is a general feeling that the Southern Confederacy will be recognized and that they deserve to be recognized."[21]

No one was more acutely aware of the army's demoralization than Lincoln. And no one had more responsibility for doing something about it. A newspaper reporter who spoke with Lincoln on August 30 had never seen the president so "wrathful" against McClellan. Lincoln seemed to think that McClellan was "a little crazy," according to his private secretary John Hay, but he agreed with Hay that "envy jealousy and spite are probably a better explanation of his present conduct."[22] Lincoln did not lack advice on what to do about the matter. Secretary of War Stanton wanted McClellan court-martialed; Secretary of the Treasury Chase said he should be shot. Four of Lincoln's Cabinet members signed a memorandum urging the president to dismiss McClellan. Secretary of the Navy Gideon Welles did not sign but agreed with the sentiments in the memorandum.[23]

Lincoln did, too, but he knew that he would have an army mutiny on his hands if he retained Pope in command. He had earlier sounded out Burnside about taking over the army, but that general declined. There seemed no alternative to McClellan. Halleck agreed. At 7:30 A.M. on September 2 Lincoln and Halleck called on McClellan at his home during breakfast and asked him to take command of all the troops as they retreated into the defenses of Washington — Pope's troops as well as his own. Three days later Lincoln expanded the order to give McClellan command of the merged armies in the field. "Again I have been called upon to save the country," McClellan wrote his wife. He accepted because "under the circumstances no one else *could* save the country."[24]

At a Cabinet meeting on September 2, Stanton and Chase vigorously opposed Lincoln's action; Chase feared "it would prove a national calamity." Two Cabinet members who kept diaries described Lincoln as "extremely distressed" during this meeting. "He seemed wrung by the bitterest anguish — said he felt ready to hang himself." And the president was not the only one who felt that way. "There was a more disturbed and desponding feeling," wrote Welles, "than I have ever witnessed in council." Lincoln agreed that McClellan "had acted badly in this matter." There was "a design, a purpose, in breaking down Pope, without regard to the consequences to the country," admitted the president. "It is shocking to see and know this." But the army was "utterly demoralized" and McClellan was the only man who could "reorganize the army and bring it out of chaos," said Lincoln. "McClellan has the army with him . . . [and] we must use the tools we have. There is no man . . . who can . . . lick these troops of ours into shape half as well as he. . . . If he can't fight himself, he excels in making others ready to fight."[25]

The memorable response of soldiers to McClellan's restoration to command confirmed Lincoln's judgment. The weather on the afternoon of September 2 was "cold and rainy" as Pope's dispirited men retreated toward Washington, recalled a veteran years later. "Everything had a look of sadness in union with our feelings. . . .

Here were stragglers plodding through the mud . . . wagons wrecked and forlorn; half-formed regiments, part of the men with guns and part without . . . while everyone you met . . . looked as if he would like to hide his head somewhere from all the world." Many soldiers then and later described what happened next. An officer mounted on a black horse with a lone escort met the first of the troops. A startled captain took one look and ran back to his colonel shouting, "General McClellan is here. 'Little Mac' is on the road." His men heard the cry. "From extreme sadness we passed in a twinkling to a delirium of delight. A Deliverer had come. . . . Men threw their caps high into the air, and danced and frolicked like schoolboys." The excitement passed quickly down the line. "Way off in the distance as he passed the different corps we could hear them cheer him. Everyone felt happy and jolly. We felt there was some chance. . . . The effect of this man's presence . . . was electrical, and too wonderful to make it worth while attempting to give a reason for it."[26] The Washington correspondent of the *Chicago Tribune*, no friend of McClellan, witnessed this demonstration. "I have disbelieved the reports of the army's affection for McClellan, being entirely unable to account for the phenomenon," he wrote. "I cannot account for it to my satisfaction now, but I accept it as a fact."[27]

McClellan brought order out of chaos and licked the troops into shape in a remarkably short time. Within a few days he had reorganized and amalgamated the disparate armies. This was perhaps his finest hour. He had gotten them ready to fight. Whether he would lead them to victory would soon be determined, for the Army of Northern Virginia had crossed the Potomac into Maryland looking for a fight.

By all the odds, Lee's victorious but worn-out army should have gone into camp for rest and refitting after Second Manassas. They had been fighting or marching almost without cessation for ten weeks. Thousands were shoeless, their uniforms were rags, and all were hungry. Although beaten, the Union army in its formidable Washington defenses had twice as many men.

But Lee was a commander who habitually defied the odds. He gave almost no thought to retreating behind the Rappahannock or into the Shenandoah Valley where his army could be resupplied. He could not stay where he was in fought-over northern Virginia denuded of supplies at the end of a long and precarious logistical umbilical cord. He had the initiative and was loath to give it up. The best chance for Confederate victory was to strike again while the enemy was "much weakened and demoralized," as Lee informed Jefferson Davis on September 3. Lee continued to believe that in a long war the greater numbers, resources, and industrial capacity of the North would prevail. Thus the South should try for a knockout punch while its armies had the power to deliver it. That time was now. Just as the Western Confederate armies were on the march in Kentucky, Lee proposed to invade Maryland, a slave state that many in the South believed to be eager to join the Confederacy, "and afford her an opportunity to throw off the oppression to which she is now subject."[28] The army could support itself from the rich, unspoiled Maryland countryside while drawing the enemy out of war-ravaged Virginia during the fall harvest. If all went well, the Army of Northern Virginia might even invade Pennsylvania and destroy the vital railroad bridge over the Susquehanna River.[29]

Without waiting for a reply to his September 3 letter to Davis, Lee ordered his troops to begin crossing the Potomac forty miles upriver from Washington on September 4. Lee was confident of Davis's approval. Equally important, as an avid reader of both Southern and Northern newspapers, he was aware of Southern enthusiasm for an invasion as well as of the dejected state of Northern opinion. "Now is the time to strike the telling and decisive blows . . . and to bring the war to a close," proclaimed the *Richmond Dispatch*. "The spirit of the army is high, the men . . . eagerly desire to avenge their ravaged country. . . . They exult in a sense of their superiority not only to the Yankees, but to any army that treads the earth." Although a good many foot-sore soldiers did not share the *Dispatch*'s sentiments, some certainly did. "If we ever expect to end" the war, wrote a lieutenant in the 4th North Carolina, "we must invade the enemies country & make him feel the evils he is inflicting on us."[30]

The North would never give up if the Confederacy remained on the defensive, agreed Southern editors. Nothing could be gained by "attempts at propitiating our enemy," wrote one. "Gen. Lee understands

Confederate cavalry leading the Army of Northern Virginia across the Potomac into Maryland on the night of September 4–5, 1862. (*Harper's Weekly*)

the Northern character well enough to know that the surest guarantee of an early peace, is the vigorous prosecution of present successes," declared another, and a third added: "If we ever have an honorable treaty of peace with the United States, it will be signed on the enemy's territory."[31]

Many Southerners could hardly believe the good news of Lee's victory at Manassas and the invasion of Maryland. "To think how it has all changed since six months ago," wrote a young woman in Virginia.

"Then, we saw nothing but disaster and destruction before us . . . and I have wondered how we ever struggled through such depths of gloom. . . . How it has all so changed I can't understand, but surely God has been with us." The "almost incredible" contrast "with the position the Confederate states occupied three months ago" had a tendency to produce euphoria. "The winter of our discontent is turned to glorious summer," exclaimed the *Richmond Examiner.*[32] Lieutenant Charles C. Jones Jr. was confident that Maryland as well as "Tennessee and Kentucky will soon be entirely relieved from the Lincoln yoke." Then "an excellent strategic point for occupation would be Harrisburg," where "Pennsylvania would furnish abundant supplies for our army, while Philadelphia, Baltimore, and Washington would be cut off from the West."[33]

Lee seemed to share this euphoria. When he learned on September 6 of Kirby Smith's capture of Richmond, Kentucky, and the occupation of Lexington and Frankfort, Lee issued a general order to his own troops announcing "this great victory" which was "simultaneous with your own at Manassas. Soldiers, press onward! . . . Let the armies of the East and West vie with each other in discipline, bravery, and activity, and our brethren of our sister States will soon be released from tyranny, and our independence be established on a sure and abiding basis." Two days later Lee issued a proclamation in Frederick "To the People of Maryland" announcing that his army had come "with the deepest sympathy [for] the wrongs that have been inflicted upon the citizens of a commonwealth allied to the States of the South by the strongest social, political, and commercial ties . . . to aid you in throwing off this foreign yoke, to enable you again to enjoy the inalienable rights of freemen."[34]

The response of Marylanders in this largely Unionist part of the state was lukewarm. But Lee was aiming even higher, at the people and government of the North. "The present posture of affairs," he wrote to Davis on September 8, "places it in [our] power . . . to propose [to the Union government] . . . the recognition of our independence." Such a proposal, coming when "it is in our power to inflict injury on our adversary . . . would enable the people of the United States to determine at their coming elections whether they will support those who favor a prolongation of the war, or those who wish to bring it to a termination."[35]

Lee's reference to "their coming elections" revealed one of the purposes of his invasion: to encourage the election of Peace Democrats to the U.S. Congress. The war had placed Northern Democrats in a difficult position. Their antebellum political power had depended on an alliance with Southern Democrats. They had traditionally sided with the South on slavery and other issues of Southern concern (those who did not had become Republicans). In 1861–62 nearly all Northern Democrats professed support for restoration of the Union. But the party soon divided into "War" and "Peace" Democrats. The former agreed with Republicans that disunion must be suppressed by military means. But they disagreed with the hard-war measures that evolved as Republican policy in 1862. They voted against confiscation and emancipation bills in Congress. They opposed Lincoln's suspension of the writ of *habeas corpus* and the military arrest of alleged Confederate sympathizers. They passed angry resolutions against such measures in their state and county conventions during 1862.

Peace Democrats opposed these measures even more vociferously. And by 1862 they also began to speak out against the war itself as a means of restoring the Union — especially the kind of war it was becoming, a war to destroy the Old South and slavery instead of a war to restore "the Union as it was." That phrase became their slogan; an armistice and peace negotiations became their policy. "Shall This War Ever Cease?" asked the title of a typical editorial in a Newark Democratic newspaper. "The people," agreed a Cincinnati Democrat, "are depressed by the interminable nature of this war." Former Governor Thomas Seymour of Connecticut considered the idea that the Union could be restored by war a "monstrous fallacy." Such convictions became stronger when the war seemed to be going badly, as it was in the late summer of 1862.[36]

Republicans likened Peace Democrats to the venomous copperhead snake, and the label "Copperhead" stuck. Republicans equated opposition to the war with support for the Confederacy and thus tarnished Copperheads with the taint of treason. They also exaggerated the Copperheads' influence in the Democratic party and tended to conflate the War Democrats' opposition to Republican war *policies* with opposition to the war itself.

But so did many Southern leaders. The *Richmond Dispatch* believed that in the North "there is a large and powerful body of citizens who are bitterly opposed to the present war."[37] That is why Lee foresaw "their coming elections" as a contest between "those who favor a prolongation of the war" (Republicans) and "those who wish to bring it to a termination" (Democrats). And termination, with Southern armies in Maryland and Kentucky, would mean Confederate independence. Thus the *New York Times* hit close to the mark when it maintained that the election of a Democratic majority in the next House of Representatives "would be regarded everywhere at the South as a symptom of *division* in the Northern States — as an indication that public sentiment had turned against the war."[38]

It would be so regarded in Europe as well. French officials, in particular, expected the Democrats to win control of the House. The French minister in Washington believed that this outcome would make the Lincoln administration amenable to mediation; he proposed that when the result of the elections became known, the

British and French should issue a joint "Manifesto" calling for mediation.[39] In England, Foreign Secretary Russell also anticipated that Lincoln would cave in if the Democrats achieved "ascendancy" in November. "I heartily wish them success," Russell added.[40]

The news of Second Manassas and of Lee's invasion accelerated the pace of intervention discussions in London and Paris. Benjamin Moran, secretary of the American legation in London, reported that "the rebels here are elated beyond measure" by tidings of Lee's victory at Manassas. Moran was disgusted by the "exultation of the British press. . . . I confess to losing my temper when I see my bleeding country wantonly insulted in her hour of disaster." Further word that Lee had invaded Maryland produced in Moran "a sense of mortification. . . . The effect of this news here, is to make those who were our friends ashamed to own the fact. . . . The Union is regarded as hopelessly gone."[41] The French foreign secretary told the American minister in Paris that these events proved "the undertaking of conquering the South is impossible." The British chancellor of the exchequer, William Gladstone, said that it was "certain in the opinion of the whole world except one of the parties . . . that the South cannot be conquered. . . . It is our absolute duty to recognise . . . that Southern independence is established."[42]

Gladstone was not a new convert to this position. The real danger to Union interests came from the potential conversion of Palmerston, who had blocked a parliamentary resolution favoring mediation two months earlier. After Second Manassas, Palmerston appeared ready to change his mind. The Federals "got a very complete smashing," he wrote to Russell (who was still abroad with Queen Victoria), "and it seems not altogether unlikely that still greater disasters await them, and that even Washington or Baltimore might fall into the hands of the Confederates." If something like that happened, "would it not be time for us to consider whether . . . England and France might not address the contending parties and recommend an arrangement on the basis of separation?" Russell needed little persuasion. He concurred, and added that if the North refused to accept mediation, "we ought ourselves to recognise the Southern States as an independent State."[43]

On September 24 (before news of

Antietam arrived in England) Palmerston informed Gladstone of the plan to hold a Cabinet meeting on the subject when Russell returned in October. The proposal would be made to both sides: "an Armistice and Cessation of the Blockades with a View to Negotiation on the Basis of Separation," to be followed by diplomatic recognition of the Confederacy.[44] But Palmerston and Russell agreed to take no action "till we see a little more into the results of the Southern invasion. . . . If the Federals sustain a great defeat . . . [their] Cause will be manifestly hopeless . . . and the iron should be struck while it is hot. If, on the other hand, they should have the best of it, we may wait a while and see what may follow."[45]

Great events therefore awaited the outcome of Lee's decision to cross the Potomac: victory or defeat; foreign intervention; Lincoln's emancipation proclamation; Northern elections; the very willingness of the Northern people to keep fighting for the Union. "Just now it does appear as if God was truly with us," wrote Major Walter Taylor, who was closer to Lee at this time than anyone else. "All along our lines the movement is onward."[46] Destiny awaited those tired, ragged, shoeless, hungry but confident Rebel soldiers on the far side of the Potomac as they forded the river singing "Maryland, My Maryland": the destiny of the Confederacy, of slavery, of the United States itself as one nation, indivisible.

Four

Showdown at Sharpsburg

The first casualty of the Confederate invasion was the anticipation that Marylanders would flock to the Southern banner. The disappointment was great, because hopes had been high. Composed the previous year by a Confederate exile from Baltimore, the words of "Maryland, My Maryland" could be sung to the familiar tune of "O Tannenbaum":

> The despot's heel is on thy shore,
> Maryland, my Maryland! . . .
> Virginia should not call in vain,
> Maryland, my Maryland!

Walter Taylor declared on September 7 that "now is the time for Maryland or never. After this if she does not rise, hush up 'My Maryland.' " A South Carolina soldier had "no dout that we will get 50000 in this state."[1]

Richmond newspapers proclaimed confidently that "the hour of Maryland's deliverance, long deferred, has come at last . . . and a noble people, long crushed under the heel of despotism, will soon have the opportunity of rising upon their tyrants." The "pride, the self-respect, and the sympathies of Maryland link her with the cause of the South. . . . The time for patriotic songs and sentimental sympathy has passed, and the hour for action has arrived." The wish soon became fact, as viewed from Richmond, with optimistic reports that large numbers of Maryland men were joining Lee's army. "This is really most gratifying news, as it gives our brilliant operations . . . a tenfold brighter promise!" proclaimed the *Richmond Enquirer*.[2]

But the reality was quite different. The reception given the invading Confederates was distinctly cool — even "cold and sinister," in the bitter words of another newspaper. At most a few score men joined the Army of Northern Virginia. A disgusted Mississippi officer wrote that " 'secesh' in Maryland was as near a humbug as anything of the day."[3] He should not have been surprised. The family farms and market towns of western Maryland, with few slaves, resembled those of Pennsylvania more than they did the farms and plantations of the South. If geography had somehow made it possible for the Confederates to cross the lower Potomac and invade tidewater Maryland, they would have found a much warmer welcome. But even in that pro-Confederate region, Lee might not have gotten many more recruits for his army, because most potential Maryland Confederate soldiers had gone south early in the war and joined Virginia regiments or formed Maryland regiments in Virginia. (The same was true in Kentucky, where Braxton Bragg's invasion of that state also generated disappointingly few recruits.)

The outward appearance of soldiers in the Army of Northern Virginia did not inspire confidence among Marylanders. Gaunt, unshaven, unwashed, their "uniforms" little more than patched and tattered rags that they had not changed or washed for weeks, they looked more like an army of beggars than of soldiers. A resident of Frederick told a reporter for the *Baltimore American* that he had smelled the army before he saw it. "I have never seen a mass of such filthy, strong-smelling men. . . . They were the roughest set of creatures

THE REBEL CHIVALRY

As the Fancy of "My Maryland" painted them.   As "My Maryland" found them.

A satirical cartoon in *Harper's Weekly* contrasting the Cavalier self-image of the Confederate "chivalry" with the reality of ragged, dirty Confederate soldiers in Maryland. (*Harper's Weekly*)

I ever saw, their features, hair, and clothing matted with dirt and filth; and the scratching they kept up gave warrant of vermin in abundance."[4] A woman in Shepherdstown, just across the Potomac from Maryland, encountered many Confederate soldiers during the campaign. "When I say that they were hungry, I convey no impression of the gaunt starvation that looked from their cavernous eyes," she later wrote. "All day they crowded to the doors of our houses, with always the same drawling complaint. 'I've been a-marchin' and a-fightin' for six weeks stiddy, and I ain't had n-a-r-thin to eat 'cept green apples an' green cawn, an' I wish you's please to gimme a bite to eat.' " This woman saw "troops march past us every summer for four years . . . but never before or after did I see anything comparable. . . . That they could march or fight at all seemed incredible."[5]

But march and fight they could, as their adversaries testified from bitter experience. "It is beyond all wonder," wrote a Union surgeon, "how such men as the rebel troops can fight as they do; that, filthy, sick, hungry, and miserable, they should prove such heroes in fight, is past explanation." Even the civilian in Frederick who smelled the army before he saw it acknowledged that "these half-fed, barefooted soldiers . . . are well-armed and equipped, and have become so inured to hardships that they care little for any of the comforts of civilization."[6]

The soldiers described here represented a sort of Darwinian survival of the fittest — the men still with the colors a week after the invasion began. Thousands did not make it that far. A striking phenomenon of this campaign was the unprecedented number of Confederate stragglers, soldiers who could not — or would not — keep up with the army. Lee launched the invasion with 55,000 men, including three divisions of reinforcements from Richmond that more than made up his losses at Second Manassas. Within a week or ten days, however, at least 10,000 men were strewn over miles of the Virginia and Maryland countryside. A few hundred of these refused to cross the Potomac because they said they had enlisted to defend the South and not to invade the North. But most had dropped out for physical rather than ideological reasons.

Lee himself branded many of the stragglers as cowards "who desert their comrades in peril" and were therefore "unworthy members of an army that has immortalized itself" in its recent campaigns.[7] Some stragglers doubtless merited Lee's harsh censure. But the stress, exhaustion, and illness produced by those campaigns were the principal causes of straggling. Some soldiers were suffering from what the World War II generation would later call "battle fatigue." Others had reached the end of their physical endurance and needed time for rest and recuperation — time that Lee's decision to invade immediately after Second Manassas did not give them. Some men who could march barefoot on Virginia's dirt roads could not do so on Maryland's macadamized pikes. The diet of green corn from roadside fields and green apples from roadside orchards laid many soldiers low with diarrhea.

Despite all these problems, however, soldiers in the Army of Northern Virginia who remained in the ranks brimmed over with confidence during their first week in Maryland. Southerners back home who read the initial glowing reports of the invasion were even more hopeful. The Confederate chief of ordnance, Josiah Gorgas, expressed assurance on September 14 that the army was "on its way to Philadelphia. We shall have to fight one more great battle . . . & then the enemy will be completely prostrate at our feet. . . . Our forces in Kentucky and Maryland are sufficient to overwhelm the foe & now is the time for audacity."[8] A Louisiana woman was certain that "we will conquer a peace" in Maryland, while a North Carolina planter's wife hoped that Lee would capture Washington "& then burn or blow up every public building in the place."[9] The *Richmond Dispatch* lampooned "the mortal

Confederate soldiers devouring green corn picked from a Maryland field. (*Battles and Leaders of the Civil War*)

terror of the Yankees" and the "Panic in Pennsylvania" as Lee's troops approached. Pennsylvanians had good reason for alarm if the editor's prescription was followed, for "we hope the troops will turn the whole country into a desert."[10]

Panic did indeed seize many Pennsylvanians during the second week of September. Farmers in southern counties took their families and drove their cattle north of the Susquehanna River. Newspapers reported "the greatest excitement" in Harrisburg and Philadelphia. The governor called out 50,000 militia. Even as far north as Wilkes-Barre (150 miles from the Maryland border) "all the church and courthouse bells rang for the people to assemble for drill." The state archives and bonds as well as the city archives and treasury funds of Philadelphia were shipped to New York. Even in that city, according to the managing editor of the *New York Tribune*, "there is the deepest anxiety . . . and a most ominous state of affairs." A prominent philanthropist in New York seriously expected that "Jeff Davis will proclaim himself Pres't of the U.S. at Harrisburg! . . . The last days of the Republic are near."[11]

Alarmist rumors, reports, and editorials abounded in normally rational Northern newspapers. The *New York World* lamented the "accumulation of disaster and disgrace that appals and sickens every heart." The pro-administration *New York Times* agreed that "disaster and humiliation" had caused "the people [to] look upon the Government at Washington as actually falling to pieces." The more sensationalist *New York Herald* predicted an Armageddon in Maryland. "If we lose it we may lose everything" and "be broken up . . . not into two confederacies, but into ten or twenty petty

178

republics of the South American school, electing each a dictator every year at the point of the bayonet, and all incessantly fighting each other."[12]

The Army of the Potomac moved out of Washington starting September 7 to seek the enemy. Many officers and men remained pessimistic despite gratitude that they were under McClellan's command again. "The *morale* of the army is much impaired by recent events," wrote General George G. Meade, commander of the Pennsylvania Reserves, one of the best divisions in the army. "I must confess I am not very sanguine of our power." The bugler of the 8th Ohio wrote on September 9 that "the soldiers have all lost faith and patriotism so the rebels have it all their own way."[13] Some soldiers had not lost faith, but even they were wishful rather than confident. "I certainly hope," wrote a private in the 2nd Vermont, "that after this campaign, we can write of something beside disaster, slaughter, defeat, and ske-daddle."[14]

As the army marched northward through Maryland, however, an almost miraculous change in morale took place. On September 8 General Alpheus Williams, a division commander in XII Corps, had

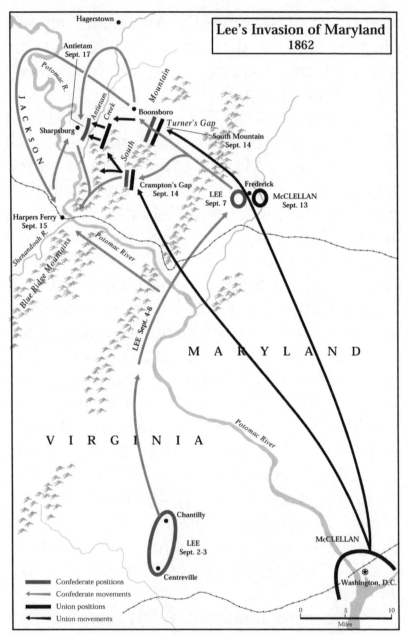

Lee's Invasion of Maryland
1862

Hagerstown

Antietam
Sept. 17

Potomac R.

JACKSON

Sharpsburg

Antietam Creek

Boonsboro

Turner's Gap

South Mountain
Sept. 14

South Mountain

Crampton's Gap
Sept. 14

LEE
Sept. 7

Frederick

McCLELLAN
Sept. 13

Harpers Ferry
Sept. 15

Shenandoah R.

Potomac River

Blue Ridge Mountains

LEE Sept. 4-6

MARYLAND

VIRGINIA

Potomac River

Chantilly

LEE
Sept. 2-3

Centreville

McCLELLAN

McCLELLAN

Washington, D.C.

Confederate positions
Confederate movements
Union positions
Union movements

0   5   10
Miles

From James M. McPherson, *Ordeal by Fire: The Civil War and Reconstruction* (New York: McGraw-Hill, 1991). By permission of The McGraw-Hill Companies.

180

written to his daughter that "we are all depressed with losses and disasters. . . . We have thrown away our power and prestige." But by September 12 he had changed his tune: "There will be a great battle or a great skedaddle on the part of the Rebels. I have great confidence that we shall smash them terribly if they stand, more confidence than I have ever had in any movement of the war."[15] This positive transformation was echoed on the home front. On September 8 Elizabeth Blair Lee, whose husband was an acting rear admiral, one brother a brigadier general, and the other postmaster general, wrote despairingly that "we are in awful times." A week later, she rejoiced that "our side begins to leap up again dont it?"[16]

What happened to cause such a change? Soldiers testified that the friendly, almost tumultuous welcome they received in Maryland boosted their spirits. This reception illustrated one of the war's ironies: instead of the Southern patriotism expected by Confederate invaders, residents of western Maryland manifested a deep-felt and unexpected American patriotism. At farm gates the farmers' daughters waited with buckets of cold spring water to quench the men's thirst. "If my hat was off once, it was off thirty times," wrote a captain whose men enjoyed the experience. "Fine marching weather," he added, "a land flowing with milk and honey; a general tone of Union sentiment among the people."[17] As the 5th Wisconsin marched through the village of Jefferson, they were "greeted with the greatest enthusiasm," wrote a private in that regiment. "Flags floated from nearly every window and ladies waved their handkerchiefs from every balcony. . . . This aroused our Patriotism which was becoming dormant." The regimental surgeon noted the "surprising change" in "the feelings and appearance of the men. The sallowness of face has given place to flush, the grumbling of dissatisfaction to joyous hilarity, the camp at night, even after our marches, resounds with mirth and music." (Perhaps there was something besides water in those buckets.)[18]

A private in the 8th Illinois Cavalry, which scouted ahead of the infantry, also marveled at the good will of Marylanders that "was so different from any thing we have met with before, that it done us so good." In the village of Middletown, the citizens "were perfectly wild. It beat all." In Boonsboro the 8th clashed with Confederate cavalry, and "tho the regiment was yelling at the top of their voices, and bullets flying like hail, the people thrust their heads from the upper windows and cheered us on."[19]

Hundreds of Union soldiers wrote enthusiastic descriptions of their reception in Frederick. The Confederates had departed only a few days earlier after cleaning out all the shoes, hats, and other clothing in town — paying in worthless Confederate currency. "When we went into Frederick, tho twas midnight we were met by *thousands*," wrote the Illinois cavalryman. "How their tongues flew, all telling wrongs suffered at the hands of the rebs." When the first Union infantry arrived next day, "an ovation awaited us that touched the inmost soul," wrote an officer. "The whole city was fluttering with Union flags."[20]

Brigade commander John Gibbon, a native of North Carolina who had remained loyal to the Union while three brothers went with the Confederacy, wrote to his wife from Maryland that "I did not believe before coming here that there was so much Union feeling in the state. . . . The whole population [of Frederick] seemed to turn out to welcome us. When Genl McClellan came thro the ladies nearly eat him up, they kissed his clothing, threw their arms around his horse's neck and committed all sorts of extravagances." Overwhelmed by the ovation, a soldier in the 8th Ohio called out to his commander: "Colonel, we're in God's country again!"[21]

This feeling of being in God's country did much to raise Union morale. "Since we have got into Maryland the health of the troops is much better as the verry air does not smell the same as it does in that God forsaken swamp," wrote a Pennsylvania soldier who had fought in the Peninsula. "Here you have good water in any quantity & plenty of fruit, corn, potatoes, tomatoes, and peaches . . . where before you could see nothing or get nothing but swamp water & then dip it out of mule tracks in the field. Thank God for the change." Captain Oliver Wendell Holmes Jr. of the 20th Massachusetts wrote to his mother on September 17, a few hours before he was severely wounded at Antietam, that "All of us feel a deuced sight more like a fight than in that forlorn Peninsula."[22]

Until September 1862 the Union army had been the invading force, fighting in enemy territory where Confederates had the advantage of knowing the terrain and defending their own turf. Now the situation was reversed and the Army of the Potomac had that edge in morale. "I am willing to fight as long as there is a man left in the 2nd Regt before I will see the North invaded," wrote a Michigan soldier. "Every man feels the necessity of doing his utmost," wrote an officer in the 57th New York. "Baltimore, Washington, and perhaps Philadelphia would be the prizes to fall into the hands of the rebels if successful, and that is surely enough to stimulate us."[23]

The Confederate invasion had cut off and isolated Harpers Ferry from Washington and from the Army of the Potomac. Lee expected the 10,500 Union troops at Harpers Ferry and 2,500 at Martinsburg to evacuate these posts, especially since their mission to protect the Baltimore and Ohio Railroad had been compromised. McClellan asked Halleck to release these troops to augment his own army. Believing that Lee's invasion force totaled 120,000, McClellan wanted all the reinforcements he could get. But Halleck refused to release these garrisons, which controlled access to and from the Shenandoah Valley, and instead ordered them to defend

Harpers Ferry "to the last extremity."[24]

This unexpected turn of events created both a problem and an opportunity for Lee. The garrison threatened his supply line through the Shenandoah Valley. At the same time, the Union base at Harpers Ferry was a rich and tempting prize: a bounty of provisions, shoes, clothing, and weapons for his needy troops — if he could capture it. On September 9, while he was at Frederick, Lee decided to try. He issued Special Orders No. 191 dividing the army into four parts. The largest part, under Jackson, was to recross the Potomac and circle around to the west of Harpers Ferry and attack it from that direction, while two other parts under Generals Lafayette McLaws and John G. Walker were to capture Maryland Heights and Loudon Heights commanding the town from the east and south. Longstreet and Lee with the remainder of the army would stay in the vicinity of Hagerstown and the gaps through the South Mountain range.

Such a division of his army ran the risk that McClellan might burst through those gaps and destroy the fragments before Lee could reunite the army. But two of Lee's hallmarks as a commander were his ability to judge an opponent's qualities and his willingness to take risks. He had twice in the last three months divided his army in the face of the enemy and gotten away with it, pouncing on the flank or rear of his adversary with his detached force. Jeb Stuart's cavalry had kept Lee informed of McClellan's cautious movements north from Washington to this date. Lee believed the Army of the Potomac to be disorganized and demoralized; he would have been surprised to learn how quickly McClellan had reorganized it. In any case, Lee considered that he had sufficient time to capture Harpers Ferry and reunite the army before the Army of the Potomac would reach South Mountain. So on September 10 the Army of Northern Virginia split up and departed from Frederick on its various missions.

Three days later the Army of the Potomac marched into Frederick greeted by delirious citizens waving flags, kissing McClellan, and hugging his horse. The 27th Indiana stopped that morning in a farm field outside of town. Corporal Barton W. Mitchell flopped down in the shade of a tree along a fenceline to enjoy a welcome rest. As he relaxed, however, Mitchell noticed a bulky envelope lying in the grass. Curious, he picked it up and discovered inside a sheet of paper wrapped around three cigars. As a comrade went off to hunt for a match so they could smoke their lucky find, Mitchell noticed that the paper contained writing under the heading "Headquarters, Army of Northern Virginia, Special Orders, No. 191," and was dated September 9. Mitchell's eyes grew wider as he read through the orders studded with names that Northern soldiers knew all too well — Jackson, Longstreet, Stuart, Hill — and was signed "R. H. Chilton, Assist. Adj.-Gen. By command of Gen. R.E. Lee."[25]

"As I read, each line became more interesting," said Mitchell later. "I forgot those cigars." (History does not record what happened to them.) Mitchell and his first sergeant John Bloss took the orders to their captain, who sent them on to his colonel, who rushed the orders to Colonel Samuel E. Pittman, division headquarters adjutant. By an extraordinary coincidence, Pittman had known R. H. Chilton before the war and, by one account, recognized his handwriting. Pittman and the division commander believed the orders to be genuine. Pittman hastened to McClellan's headquarters and showed him the document. "Now I know what to do!"

exclaimed McClellan. General Gibbon, who was present, quoted the army commander as saying: "Here is a paper with which if I cannot whip 'Bobbie Lee,' I will be willing to go home."[26]

The odds against the occurrence of such a chain of events must have been a million to one. Yet they happened. No one knows how the orders came to be wrapped around three cigars and then lost. Chilton had prepared seven copies for the various commanders whose duties were spelled out therein, plus one for headquarters files. The lost copy was addressed to Major-General Daniel Harvey Hill, whose division had joined the army after Second Manassas. Hill's division had come under Jackson's command but would be detached from it for this operation. Unaware that Hill had been sent a separate copy, Jackson had another one made and delivered to him. Hill received that copy, but not the one from Lee's headquarters, which was the one Mitchell found in the field.

Whatever was the true story of how these orders had been lost, McClellan was granted a windfall such as few generals in history have enjoyed. It was a remarkable example of the contingencies that change the course of history. As Major Walter

Taylor of Lee's staff later wrote, "the loss of this battle order constitutes one of the pivots on which turned the event of the war." At noon on September 13, McClellan wired President Lincoln: "I think Lee has made a gross mistake, and that he will be severely punished for it. . . . I have the plans of the rebels, and will catch them in their own trap."[27]

But McClellan was determined to be careful. No rashness. After all, in McClellan's mind the Rebels outnumbered him by 40,000 men (in reality, the disparity was almost the opposite). Thus he must move cautiously. Six hours passed before McClellan issued the first orders to the commanders who were to march to the South Mountain gaps and attack the divided enemy. And when were they to march? Immediately? No, tomorrow morning would do. One can readily imagine what would have happened if the situation had been reversed and Lee had discovered that McClellan's army was split into four parts too distant from each other for mutual support. He would have had Jackson on the march within the hour, with Longstreet right behind. The first Union troops did not move until eighteen hours after McClellan had seen Lee's orders.

And that was all the margin Lee needed to avert disaster.

September 14 was an eventful day. The Union garrison at Martinsburg had retreated to Harpers Ferry, followed closely by Jackson's three divisions, which moved into position on Schoolhouse Ridge that day. Located at the confluence of the Shenandoah and Potomac Rivers and virtually surrounded by high hills, Harpers Ferry was a trap waiting to be sprung by any force that could get artillery onto those heights. Commander of the Union garrison there, now swollen to 13,000 men by the Martinsburg contingent, was Colonel Dixon Miles of Maryland. Miles had commanded a small division at First Bull Run, where he was drunk. Denied promotion and nursing grievances, Miles was shunted off to this backwater command where he proceeded to prove that the court of inquiry which had reprimanded him for drunkenness and incompetence had been right.

To compound Miles's problems, most of his troops were new regiments with little training and no combat experience. The only way to defend Harpers Ferry was to prevent an enemy from occupying the heights. But Miles sent nobody across the

A wartime photograph of Harpers Ferry (after the railroad bridge was rebuilt) showing how vulnerable it was to the commanding Maryland Heights across the Potomac River on the left and Loudon Heights across the Shenandoah River on the right. (National Archives)

Shenandoah to Loudon Heights, which was seized by a Confederate division on September 12. To Maryland Heights across the Potomac he sent only 1,600 men, half of them new troops who broke and ran when two veteran Southern brigades attacked on September 13. Maryland Heights and its commanding position fell to the Confederates.

On September 14 Jackson tightened the

noose around Harpers Ferry and Confederate artillery began firing at the garrison trapped like fish in a barrel. Jackson sent a message to Lee that he expected to capture the whole garrison the next day. That night 1,200 Union cavalry escaped on an unguarded road north along the Potomac, and even managed to capture some of Longstreet's reserve ammunition wagons next morning. But that morning Harpers Ferry did indeed surrender. Miles's defense had been so inept as to arouse suspicions of treason. But he never had to answer such a charge, for he was mortally wounded in the last exchange of fire before the surrender. As Jackson rode past the captured Union troops dressed as usual in his dusty, nondescript uniform and battered fatigue cap, one soldier said, "Boys, he's not much for looks, but if we'd had him we wouldn't have been caught in this trap."[28]

The good news from Harpers Ferry was especially welcome to Lee, for on other fronts the events of September 14 had gone against him. If McClellan had moved more quickly on the 13th he might have taken Lee more completely by surprise. But that night Lee received a dispatch from Stuart notifying him of unusual bustle in the Army of the Potomac. A citizen of Frederick, a Confederate sympathizer, happened to be present at McClellan's headquarters when the general saw Lee's Orders No. 191. The citizen, whose name is lost to history, realized that something out of the ordinary had occurred and hastened through Confederate lines to find Stuart, who in turn notified Lee at Hagerstown. Anticipating a Union drive through the South Mountain passes, Lee prepared to defend them. When the Army of the Potomac's IX Corps and I Corps advanced on Turner's Gap (and nearby Fox's Gap) and VI Corps moved against Crampton's Gap on the 14th, they found Confederate troops holding the passes.

These defenders were badly outnumbered. But they occupied strong positions among the woods, rocks, and fencelines that flanked the defiles. During a long day of fighting at Fox's and Turner's Gaps in which D. H. Hill's division bore the brunt of battle, Lee and Longstreet managed to get nearly 14,000 men into action. They hung on desperately until dark against an attacking force that eventually built up to 28,000 men. When night ended the fighting, both Confederate flanks had caved in and the position had become untenable. The Confederates lost between 1,900 and 2,700 men and the Federals 1,813.[29]

Meanwhile a half-dozen miles to the south, General William B. Franklin finally got 9,000 men of VI Corps in position to storm Crampton's Gap in midafternoon. They smashed through the thin line of 2,150 defending Confederates, who suffered 962 casualties while inflicting 533 on the attackers. McClellan had ordered Franklin to push on to relieve the besieged Miles at Harpers Ferry. But Franklin advanced cautiously and stopped at dusk when he encountered Confederate reinforcements in the valley between South Mountain and Maryland Heights. By next morning, of course, it was too late to save Harpers Ferry.

On the night of September 14–15 the Confederate situation seemed dire. Southern casualties that day amounted to almost a quarter of all troops that were not besieging Harpers Ferry. Jackson's courier announcing the imminent capture of that place had not yet reached Lee. The Confederate commander knew that the whole Army of the Potomac would pour through the gaps next day. To save his own army,

Lee believed it necessary to retreat to Virginia and abandon the campaign. At 8:00 P.M. he sent a courier to General McLaws with this dispatch: "The day has done against us and this army will go by Sharpsburg to cross the river." McLaws was to pull out and recross the Potomac as well. D. H. Hill and Longstreet withdrew their troops from Turner's Gap and headed for Sharpsburg and a nearby ford over the river.[30]

At 9:40 that evening McClellan sent a telegram to Washington announcing "a glorious victory" and followed it the next morning with two more dispatches reporting that the enemy was retreating "in a perfect panic, & that Genl. Lee last night stated publicly that he must admit they had been shockingly whipped. . . . It is stated that Lee gives his loss as 15000."[31] It is not likely that Lee said anything of the sort, nor were the Confederates retreating in panic. Nevertheless, McClellan's dispatches appeared in Northern newspapers on September 16, accompanied by exuberant editorial commentary. The South Mountain battles "turn back the tide of rebel successes," crowed the *New York World*. "The strength of the rebels is hopelessly broken" and the country had been rescued "from the most imminent and deadly peril to which it has ever been exposed." The staunchly Unionist *Baltimore American* declared: "Our army has proved itself like that god of ancient mythology who gained strength from contact with his mother earth, and rises from a fall prepared with a new fund of resolution and stamina." To which the *New York Herald* added: "Now Forward to Richmond."[32]

McClellan's hyperbole would come back to haunt him. For the moment, however, all looked rosy. On September 15 Lincoln wired McClellan: "God bless you, and all with you. Destroy the rebel army, if possible."[33] Neither McClellan nor Lincoln knew as they exchanged these dispatches that Harpers Ferry had surrendered and that Lee had reconsidered his decision to retreat. That decision had been a bitter pill. If he left Maryland after the South Mountain defeats on September 14, he would be admitting failure. All of his own expectations and those of the Southern people would come crashing down. The Confederacy's best hope for victory in the war — the dual invasions of Maryland and Kentucky — would collapse if Lee had to retreat from Maryland. Lee's spirits on the night of September 14–15 were lower than at any time since he had taken command of the Army of Northern Virginia. But at sunrise on the 15th, Jackson's courier finally found Lee and delivered the message anticipating the surrender of Harpers Ferry that very day.[34]

As he read this dispatch, the sun also rose in Lee's soul. It changed everything. The invasion of Maryland could continue. Reinforced by the divisions that had captured Harpers Ferry, Lee could challenge McClellan to the war-winning battle he had sought when he came north. Jackson's courier reached Lee near Sharpsburg, where a line of ridges ran through a rural landscape of pastures, crop fields, and woodlots from the Potomac three miles north of the village to Antietam Creek a mile and a half southeast of it. "We will make our stand on these hills," Lee informed his subordinates.[35] It was a good defensive position with both flanks anchored on water. It had one disadvantage — the only route of retreat was a single ford over the Potomac three miles to the rear. But Lee was willing to take that risk to salvage his campaign, confident that when reunited his veterans would wrest victory from the Federal jaws.

An illustration from *Harper's Weekly* (detail) depicting contrabands captured by Confederate soldiers being driven back to Virginia and slavery. (*Harper's Weekly*)

At noon on the 15th a second courier rode up to Lee with word from Jackson that Harpers Ferry had indeed surrendered. Messages went out to Lee's scattered units: march to Sharpsburg as fast as you can. They did, except for General Ambrose Powell Hill's division, which remained at Harpers Ferry to parole the 12,000 Union captives and to secure the valuable spoils of war the Confederates had captured. (Those spoils included at least 500 contrabands who had found refuge with the Federals but were returned to slavery by their Confederate captors.)[36] Until these reinforcements arrived, Lee would have fewer than 18,000 men to face the oncoming Yankees. As usual, however, McClellan assumed that Lee had more than twice that number. On the afternoon of September 15 McClellan arrived on the east side of Antietam Creek but launched no probing attacks and sent no cavalry reconnaissance across the two undefended bridges or the several fords to determine Confederate strength.

On the 16th McClellan had 55,000 troops on hand with another 14,000 within six miles. Lee's force had not yet increased to much more than 25,000. Having informed Washington three days earlier that he would crush Lee's army while it was separated, McClellan had missed his first opportunity to do so on the 14th. He missed his second chance on the 16th as he spent much of the day planning an attack on September 17 — by which time all of the Army of Northern Virginia would be united except for A. P. Hill's division. Without Hill, Lee had 36,000 men, which McClellan tripled in his mind.

McClellan considered his own soldiers

to be in "excellent spirits," however, and in that respect, at least, he was right.[37] Their victory at South Mountain and McClellan's own remarkable charisma had pumped up their morale. The colonel of the 10th Pennsylvania Reserves testified to the tonic effect of victory. This regiment had fought well but suffered heavy losses on the Peninsula and at Second Bull Run. Tired, sullen, and more than a little gun-shy, they went into action at Turner's Gap without spirit, and "hung back in a way they had never done before," their colonel reported. He finally got them to attack across a ravine. "Soon nearly all were in the ravine and . . . the rebels were running. . . . In a few minutes confidence took the place of hesitation and all pressed wildly forward driving the enemy" and capturing many prisoners. That night the colonel was still so excited that though exhausted he could not sleep. "I never felt before as then," he wrote. "The stars looked as though they were made partakers of our glory. . . . The consciousness that we had by sheer hard fighting, beaten the enemy and driven him from his strong positions filled me to overflowing and gave me con-fidence that we would finally win."[38]

An incident on the evening of September

16 bespoke McClellan's charisma. As a New York artillery battery arrived at its designated place in the line, McClellan and his staff rode by them. "What do you suppose 'Little Mac' did?" wrote one of the battery's lieutenants. "Why he saluted every driver individually, and every cannoneer, if marching singly, in the same way. And he did it with that pleasant smile of his, which has been so often remarked." Which "of our other great generals ever did this?" asked the lieutenant. "Soldiers have written, and are writing constantly about the enthusiasm manifested at the sight of McClellan. It is all true. . . . They love him, they trust him, and they will follow him no matter where he leads."[39]

The problem was that he too seldom led. But on the late afternoon of the 16th McClellan sent his most aggressive corps commander, "Fighting Joe" Hooker, across the Antietam northeast of Sharpsburg. Joseph Mansfield's XII Corps followed Hooker's I Corps. McClellan's intention was for these two corps, supported by Edwin V. Sumner's II Corps, to attack the Confederate left. Once these troops were engaged, McClellan expected Ambrose Burnside's IX Corps to fight its way across the Antietam on the Confederate right and cut off Lee's retreat route to the Potomac ford. McClellan planned to keep the two divisions of Fitz-John Porter's V Corps and the two arriving divisions of Franklin's VI Corps in reserve to exploit any Union breakthrough or contain any Confederate counterattack. Curiously, McClellan also kept his large cavalry division in reserve in the center, apparently with some Napoleonic notion of a grand mounted charge against broken and fleeing Confederates. He should have sent at least some horsemen to patrol and protect the flanks. His failure to do so would have unhappy consequences for the Union left on September 17.

Except for the cavalry disposition, it was a good battle plan — if well executed. But it was not well executed because the various attacks occurred seriatim, division by division, instead of going forward in coordinated fashion. The chief fault was McClellan's, for it was his job to coordinate them. His negligence in this matter enabled Lee to shift his badly outnumbered defenders (McClellan had about 75,000 effectives) from one sector to another to meet the greatest threats. Never during that long, bloody day from dawn to dusk did McClellan get more than 20,000 men into action at the same time; 20,000 of his soldiers did not fire a shot at all.

After crossing the Antietam on September 16, Hooker's vanguard got into a firefight with several Confederate regiments in what came to be known in the geography of the battle as the East Woods. The skirmish died away after dark, having alerted Lee to the point of attack the next morning. The opposing armies settled down for a restless, nervous night under a light rain that soon ceased. A newspaper reporter with Hooker's corps heard the general say: "We are through for the night . . . but tomorrow we fight the battle that will determine the fate of the Republic." General Alpheus Williams, commander of a division in XII Corps, wrote a few days later that he would never forget that night, "so dark, so obscure, so mysterious, so uncertain . . . there was a half-dreamy sensation about it all; but with a certain impression that the morrow was to be great with the future fate of our country."[40]

Hooker's troops seemed animated by the same sentiments, for they attacked at dawn with unprecedented élan. Sweeping south on both sides of the Hagerstown Pike into a cornfield and through the East Woods, they fought with savage fury. The Confederates in this sector, commanded by Jackson, gave as good as they got. Major Rufus Dawes of the 6th Wisconsin described the action in this sector between 6:00 and 7:00 A.M. "Men, I can not say fell; they were knocked out of the ranks by dozens. But we jumped over the fence, and pushed on, loading, firing, and shouting as we advanced. There was, on the part of the men, great hysterical excitement, eagerness to go forward, and a reckless disregard of life, of everything but victory." So vivid were Dawes's memories of this action that he suddenly switched to the present tense: "The men are loading and firing with demoniacal fury and shouting and laughing hysterically, and the whole field before us is covered with rebels fleeing for life, into the woods. Great numbers of them are shot while climbing over the high post and rail fences along the turnpike."[41]

Dawes's regiment fought mainly in a thirty-acre cornfield. So did dozens of other regiments on both sides, back and forth in attacks and counterattacks for several hours, until the field was filled with so many dead and wounded men that, as many soldiers who fought there put it (doubtless with some exaggeration), one could walk through the field without ever

Louisiana soldiers fighting along the fenceline bordering the Hagerstown Pike north of Sharpsburg on the morning of September 17. For the aftermath of this action, see the photograph on page 15 of this book. (*Battles and Leaders of the Civil War*)

stepping on the ground. Many cornfields were the scene of fighting during the Civil War, but this one was ever after known as *the* Cornfield. "In the time I am writing, every stalk of corn in the northern and greater part of the field was cut as closely as with a knife," wrote Hooker in his official report, "and the slain lay in rows precisely as they had stood in their ranks a few minutes before. It was never my fortune to witness a more bloody, dismal battlefield."[42]

Hooker's three divisions fought alone,

without support, for an hour and a half while Jackson and Lee also fed three divisions into the meat grinder. One of them was perhaps the hardest fighting outfit in the Army of Northern Virginia, commanded by John Bell Hood. This division had just been issued its first rations in three days and had retired to the rear to cook them when Jackson urgently ordered the men forward to stem a Union breakthrough at the south end of the cornfield. "Just as we began to cook our rations near daylight," wrote a Georgia soldier in a diary entry next day, "we were shelled and ordered into formation. I have never seen a more disgusted bunch of boys and mad as hornets."[43]

Infuriated by this interruption of their breakfast, Hood's veterans hurtled forward with a wild rebel yell and smashed the Yankees, only to be counterattacked and smashed in turn. "Never have I seen men fall as fast and thick," wrote a South Carolinian who was wounded in this action. "In about one hour's time our whole division was almost annihilated." One of Hood's regiments, the 1st Texas, lost 82 percent of its men in forty-five minutes of fighting. The regimental commander (who survived) described an incident during this action: "Major Matt Dale, commanding the right wing, came to me at my station at the center and reported that nearly every man of the right wing had been shot down," and "not a man would be left alive unless we withdrew at once. The roar all about us of nearby small arms and of artillery more distant was so deafening that the Major . . . had to place his mouth at my ear. Just as he concluded and whilst we still were standing breast to breast . . . he was stricken with a bullet, straightened, stiffened, and fell backwards prone upon the ground, dead." When an unstrung Hood met with Lee later that night he informed the commander that "my division has been almost wiped out."[44]

If McClellan had managed to get the two divisions of XII Corps to attack along with Hooker's I Corps, he might have rolled up Lee's left flank. But XII Corps did not go into action until Hooker's men were pretty well fought out, enabling Lee to shift parts of three fresh divisions to meet this new attack. One XII Corps brigade penetrated to the small church of the Dunkard (or Dunker) sect, a landmark on the battlefield, but this potential breakthrough was also unsupported. By this time General Mansfield, commander of

XII Corps, had been mortally wounded and Hooker had also been put out of action with a wound.

In keeping with the pattern of serial attacks, McClellan finally ordered Sumner's II Corps to cross the creek and assault the Confederate position in what became known as the West Woods. Sixty-four years old, "Bull" Sumner was known more for persistence than brilliance. He rode forward with his lead division, commanded by General John Sedgwick. Moving in a tight column of brigades to increase their battering-ram power, Sedgwick's division marched through part of the devastated cornfield, crossed the Hagerstown Pike, and penetrated to the western edge of the West Woods almost without opposition. A private in the most advanced regiment, the 15th Massachusetts, described what happened next. "The rebs all began to fall back. Good said I, we have got um now. . . . But at the same instant I heard a cry from the rear, 'Fall Back . . . we are flanked on our left, the rebs are getting in our rear.' What. Great God can't be possible. But I saw it was no joke, the bullets actually came from the rear." Sedgwick's division had marched into an ambush by two fresh enemy divi-

A Union attack near the Dunkard church mid-morning of September 17. For the aftermath of this action, see the photograph on page 15 of this book. (*Battles and Leaders of the Civil War*)

sions that had been shifted from other sectors, plus remnants of other divisions, who popped up from behind bushes, trees, fencelines, and limestone outcroppings to pour a devastating fire into the Union front, flank, and rear. "My God, such confusion," wrote the 15th Massachusetts soldier. "All hands ran for dear life. The rebs chased us like the Devil. . . . No God Damned Southerner is a going to catch me unless he can run 29 miles an hour."[45]

This soldier was luckier than 334 other

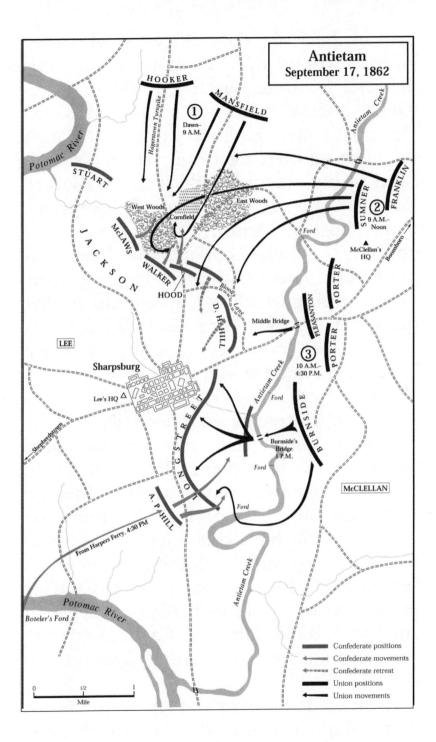

Antietam
September 17, 1862

HOOKER

MANSFIELD

①
Dawn–
9 A.M.

Hagerstown Turnpike

Antietam Creek

Potomac River

STUART

West Woods

East Woods

Cornfield

FRANKLIN

SUMNER

②
9 A.M.–
Noon

McClellan's
HQ

Ford

Boonsboro

J A C K S O N

McLAWS

WALKER

HOOD

Bloody Lane

D. H. HILL

PORTER

PLEASANTON

PORTER

Middle Bridge

③
10 A.M.–
4:30 P.M.

LEE

Sharpsburg

Lee's HQ

L O N G S T R E E T

Antietam Creek

Ford

BURNSIDE

Ford

Burnside's
Bridge
1 P.M.

Ford

McCLELLAN

Shepherdstown

A. P. HILL

Ford

From Harpers Ferry, 4:30 PM

Potomac River

Boteler's Ford

Antietam Creek

	Confederate positions
	Confederate movements
	Confederate retreat
	Union positions
	Union movements

0   1/2   1
Mile

men in the 15th Massachusetts, who were killed, wounded, or missing in this debacle. So were another 1,700 in Sedgwick's division. One of the wounded was Oliver Wendell Holmes Jr., shot through the neck and left for dead. (He recovered, lived to his ninety-fourth year, and served for thirty-three of those years as a Supreme Court justice.) Another wounded Massachusetts soldier, shot in the knee, remained helpless in no-man's land for many hours, during which he wrote in his pocket diary: "Battle Oh horrid battle What sights I have seen now see around me I am wounded! And am afraid shall be again as shells fly past me every few seconds . . . Am in severe pain how the shells fly I do sincerely hope shall not be wounded again."[46] He was eventually rescued and his leg amputated, but he died at the end of September — one of twelve thousand casualties (on both sides) in four hours of the war's most intense combat on the Confederate left. Five Union and four Confederate divisions were so badly wrecked that they backed off almost as if by mutual consent and did no more serious fighting that day.

Meanwhile Sumner's other two divisions had obliqued to the south to attack parts of two Confederate divisions holding Lee's center along a half mile of a farm road where generations of wagons hauling grain to a mill had worn ruts that eroded the road several feet below ground level. This ready-made trench was an exceptionally strong defensive position. Wave after wave of brigade-size Union attacks were beaten back, with the famous Irish Brigade taking especially heavy punishment but dealing out just as much in return.

Four hours of action on this front left a carpet of blue-clad corpses strewn across the fields northeast of the sunken road and a carpet of butternut and gray-clad corpses in the appropriately named Bloody Lane. Once again, as many soldiers testified and photographs proved, one could walk along the road without touching the ground. About 1:00 P.M. the Yankees finally broke through and cleared Bloody Lane of all surviving unwounded Rebels. Lieutenant Thomas Livermore of the 5th New Hampshire, one of the Federal units that scored the breakthrough, described the final moments of this action. "As the fight grew furious, the colonel cried out, 'Put on the war paint,'" recalled Livermore. "We rubbed the torn end of the cartridges over our faces, streaking them with powder like

Confederate dead in Bloody Lane after the fighting there at midday September 17. Photograph by Alexander Gardner on September 19. (Library of Congress)

a pack of Indians, and the colonel . . . cried out, 'Give 'em the war whoop!' and all of us joined him in the Indian war whoop until it must have rung out above all the thunder of the ordnance."[47]

The broken Southern brigades fell back in disorder almost half a mile. Lee's center was wide open except for some artillery and a handful of dazed infantrymen that Confederate officers including Longstreet desperately scraped together back along the Hagerstown Pike. "There was no body of Confederate infantry in this part of the field that could have resisted a serious advance," wrote a Southern officer. "Lee's army was ruined," added Longstreet's artillery commander melodramatically, "and the end of the Confederacy was in sight."[48] Now was the time for McClellan to send in his reserves. Longstreet himself later said that if 10,000 fresh Union troops had been put in at that juncture, the Confederates would have been swept from the field.[49]

McClellan had those 10,000 available in Franklin's corps, and several thousand more in Porter's. The normally cautious Franklin pleaded to be unleashed. But Sumner, who was still shocked by what had happened to Sedgwick's division, counseled against it. Fearing that Lee must be massing his own supposedly abundant reserves for a counterattack, McClellan accepted Sumner's advice. "It would not be prudent to make the attack," he told Franklin.[50] So the opportunity passed, Lee and Longstreet patched together a new line along the Hagerstown Pike, and this sector of the battlefield fell quiet.

Meanwhile what of Burnside on the

Union left? His IX Corps had been augmented by the temporary attachment of the "Kanawha Division" that had helped win West Virginia for the Union during the previous year. One of the regiments in this division, the 23rd Ohio, would eventually possess a distinction shared by no other military unit in history: it contained two future presidents of the United States, Lieutenant-Colonel Rutherford B. Hayes and Sergeant William McKinley. Hayes had been wounded at South Mountain three days earlier and was not present at Antietam; the nineteen-year-old McKinley was regimental commissary sergeant at this time. (McKinley's excellent four-year war record is not fairly represented by the monument at Antietam, which praises him for serving coffee to the troops under fire.)

McClellan had told Burnside to hold his corps ready for an early attack across Antietam Creek. But as the hours passed and the fighting rose to a dreadful crescendo in the Cornfield and West Woods on the Confederate left, no orders came. Lee was able to shift one division and an additional brigade from his right to the left because of lack of action on Burnside's front; these Confederate units played a major role in the ambush of Sedgwick's division. Finally, about 10:00 A.M., orders arrived from McClellan for Burnside to attack. The subsequent lethargy and ineptness of Burnside's operations did much to erode the good reputation he had earned thus far in the war.

After the departure of reinforcements to the left, Lee had fewer than 4,000 men to defend against Burnside's 13,000. The Confederates held high ground commanding the Antietam, however, with heavy woods and an abandoned quarry overlooking the only bridge and providing cover for two Georgia regiments that poured a lethal fire on anything trying to cross the bridge. Even though the thirty-yard wide Antietam was shallow and fordable at several places, Burnside seemed fixated on the bridge. The general was in a peevish mood. His friendship with McClellan had recently cooled; McClellan may have been aware that Lincoln had twice sounded out Burnside about taking command of the army. During the march from Washington to the vicinity of Sharpsburg, Burnside had commanded the left wing of the advance, including Hooker's corps as well as his own. Burnside now seemed to be sulking because McClellan had removed Hooker from his

The Union attack across "Burnside's Bridge" about 1 P.M. on September 17. (*Frank Leslie's Illustrated History of the Civil War*)

control for the battle.

Whatever the reason, Burnside showed little energy and less imagination in his tactical dispositions. For three hours various IX Corps regiments tried in piecemeal fashion to fight their way across the Rohrbach Bridge, which ever since has been known as Burnside's Bridge. Nothing worked. Finally, about 1:00 P.M., one small Union division crossed at a ford a mile downstream. At the same time a Pennsylvania and a New York regiment (the latter containing Lieutenant George Whitman,

Attack by the 9th New York "Zouaves" to the outskirts of Sharpsburg on the afternoon of September 17. (*Frank Leslie's Illustrated History of the Civil War*)

brother of Walt Whitman) attacked directly across the bridge, taking their losses, clearing out the Georgia defenders and establishing a bridgehead for the rest of the corps. But then another unnecessary delay occurred as the lead division had to go back for ammunition that should have been brought forward earlier.

At 3:00 P.M. Burnside at last got his whole line moving forward across the hills and fields south of Sharpsburg. The Federal unit that penetrated farthest was the 9th New York, one of the colorful

"Zouave" regiments still dressed in the bright red baggy trousers and tasseled fezzes that had been popular in the war's first year. The 9th fought its way through a heavy fire. Lieutenant Matthew Graham described a moment during the advance. "I was lying on my back . . . watching the shells explode and speculating as to how long I could hold up my finger before it would be shot off," he wrote, "for the very air seemed full of bullets, when the order to get up was given, I turned over quickly to look at Col. Kimball, who had given the order, thinking he had suddenly become insane." Up they got, though, and moved forward. Graham was wounded at the climax of the assault, by which time the whole color guard had been killed or wounded. "One or two of the men staggered to their feet and reached for the colors, but were shot down at once," wrote Graham. "Then there was what seemed a spontaneous rush for them by a dozen or more men from several companies, who were shot down in succession as each one raised his flag. . . . The flags were up and down, several times a minute."[51]

A literary-minded private in the same regiment, David Thompson, described the mental and physical stress of such intense combat as the 9th New York experienced at Antietam. "The truth is," Thompson confessed, "when bullets are whacking against tree-trunks and solid shot are cracking skulls like egg-shells, the consuming passion in the breast of the average man is to get out of the way." But he too got up and went forward when the order came. "In a second the air was full of the hiss of bullets and the hurtle of grape-shot. The mental strain was so great that I saw at that moment the singular effect mentioned, I think, in the life of Goethe on a similar occasion — the whole landscape for an instant turned slightly red."[52]

The Confederates put up a stiff resistance but the sheer weight of numbers forced them back to the edge of Sharpsburg. By about 4:00 P.M. it appeared that Burnside would capture the Harpers Ferry Road south of town and cut Lee's only route of retreat to the Potomac ford. At this moment of supreme crisis, Lee looked south anxiously toward his crumbling flank. He saw a cloud of dust that soon materialized into a column of marching men. "Whose troops are those?" Lee asked a nearby lieutenant with a telescope. The lieutenant peered intently for what seemed an eternity, then said: "They are flying the

Virginia and Confederate flags, sir."
Uttering a sigh of relief, Lee said: "It is
A. P. Hill from Harpers Ferry."[53]

Indeed it was. The previous night Lee
had sent a courier to Hill ordering him to
finish up the surrender arrangements and
get his division to Sharpsburg as soon as
possible. Hill had his men on the road by
7:30 A.M. on the 17th. His forced march of
seventeen miles left hundreds of stragglers
strewn along the way, but enough men got
to Sharpsburg to save the day. If
McClellan had placed some of his cavalry
on the flank they could have detected
Hill's approach in time to send warning.

Hill crashed into Burnside's flank and
rolled it up. The regiment on the far left
was the 16th Connecticut, one of the new
regiments organized in response to Lincoln's July 1 call for volunteers. Never
having fired a shot in anger — indeed,
having scarcely fired their rifles even in
training — and with no experience of
maneuvering under fire, the 16th collapsed
almost immediately, creating a domino
effect on other Union regiments as the
16th's broken ranks fled to the rear. Some
of Hill's men had exchanged their rags for
new blue uniforms they had seized at
Harpers Ferry and carried a captured

American flag as a ruse, which compounded confusion on the flank as some Union soldiers held their fire thinking that Hill's men were friends.

The 16th Connecticut's experience also illustrated a problem that had occurred elsewhere on this deadly day. About 15 percent of the Union soldiers who saw action were new recruits. Their training had been brief and superficial. Although willing and even enthusiastic, they probably harmed rather than helped the Union cause.[54]

Despite the collapse of his left, the right flank of Burnside's attack still had plenty of momentum that threatened to break through a thin Confederate line directly east of Sharpsburg (where the national cemetery is now located). Here was another opportunity for McClellan to send in his reserves. He had earlier promised Burnside support if he needed it. Most of Porter's V Corps as well as the cavalry were nearby and available. Several V Corps officers wanted to pitch in, and McClellan seemed inclined to approve. But a V Corps division commander heard Porter say to McClellan: "Remember, General! I command the last reserve of the last Army of the Republic." This reminded McClellan of those phantom reserves of Lee's, whose existence perhaps seemed confirmed by the arrival of A. P. Hill. Porter later denied the report of this incident, but his denial is not persuasive. And most of his corps did remain idle. A civilian at McClellan's headquarters overheard staff officers estimate that Lee had 125,000 men at Sharpsburg. McClellan and Porter apparently believed the same. So Burnside's attack was unsupported and Lee's line unbroken.[55]

Night fell on a scene of horror beyond imagining: 2,108 Union dead and estimates ranging from 1,546 to 2,700 Confederate dead on the battlefield; 9,549 Union wounded and estimates of 7,752 to 9,024 Confederate wounded.[56] Of the wounded on both sides, at least two thousand would die of their wounds. The detritus of battle lay thickly on the field: smashed weapons and gun carriages, dead horses, scraps of bloody clothing, discarded knapsacks and blanket rolls, and the smell of rotting corpses, vomit, and excrement. "No tongue can tell, no mind can conceive, no pen portray the horrible sights I witnessed" as the sun rose next morning, a Pennsylvania soldier wrote in his diary.[57]

The sun also rose on some 30,000 alive and unwounded Confederate soldiers still in line as if to dare the Yankees to renew the attack. In truth, most on both sides expected the battle to resume. So, apparently, did McClellan, for at 8:00 A.M. he wired Halleck that "the battle will probably be renewed today."[58] During the day McClellan received 13,000 reinforcements, which with the 20,000 who had remained in reserve the previous day gave him more fresh troops than Lee had men in his whole force. In view of McClellan's pre-battle estimate of 110,000 or more Confederates, however, he assumed that Lee's forces still outnumbered his own.

The more McClellan thought about it, the more he believed that there was no "reasonable certainty of success if I renewed the attack," as he put it in a preliminary report on October 15. In his final report written almost a year later, he used similar language: "I concluded that the success of an attack on the 18th was not certain. . . . I should have had a narrow view of the condition of the country had I been willing to hazard another battle with less than an absolute assurance of success."[59]

There we have McClellan in a nutshell

— he would take no initiative without "absolute assurance of success" — which rarely if ever exists in any human endeavor, much less in war. So the long day of Thursday, September 18 wore away with only sporadic picket firing as burial squads began their grisly task and Lee prepared to retreat across the Potomac after dark. That night the Army of Northern Virginia got clean away. In his diary a captain in the 18th Georgia wrote that he was glad to go, "for I have seen all of this state I care to for a life time."[60]

McClellan was delighted to see them go. Next morning he wired Halleck: "Our victory was complete. The enemy is driven back into Virginia."[61] But some Union soldiers did not agree that the victory was complete. "We should have followed them up the next day," wrote a captain from Maine on September 21. A Connecticut officer could "imagine no earthly reason why we did not go at them the next day with a vengeance." And Colonel Thomas Welsh, who commanded a IX Corps brigade that had done some of the best fighting in that corps, expressed himself (privately) "thoroughly disgusted with the management of this army. . . . The whole Rebel Army could have been captured or destroyed easily before it could have crossed the Potomac — but indeed it seems to me that McClellan let them escape purposely."[62]

On September 20 McClellan did send several V Corps regiments across the Potomac in a feeble pursuit that was easily repulsed by A. P. Hill's division, accomplishing nothing more than to lengthen the casualty list. In Washington, Gideon Welles wrote in his diary on September 19: "Nothing from the army, except that, instead of following up the victory, attacking and capturing the Rebels, they . . . are rapidly escaping across the river. . . . Oh dear."[63] Welles's sentiments undoubtedly echoed those of Lincoln, who four days earlier had prodded McClellan to "destroy the rebel army, if possible."

McClellan was irritated by the lack of praise or recognition from Washington for his great victory. "I feel some little pride," he wrote, "in having with a beaten and demoralized army defeated Lee so utterly, & saved the North so completely. Well — one of these days history will I trust do me justice."[64] History can at least do him the justice to say that he did indeed take a beaten and demoralized army and turn it again into an efficient fighting machine —

even if he was reluctant to run this machine at full speed for fear of breaking it. And perhaps he did save the North, or at least stop the downward spiral of Northern morale. But the war would go on for two and one-half more years, and it would be left to others to "defeat Lee utterly."

Five

The Beginning of the End

The Army of Northern Virginia was not destroyed at Antietam, as Lincoln had hoped. Nor was it beaten utterly, as McClellan claimed. But it was badly hurt. Three of the nine division commanders, nineteen of thirty-six brigade commanders, and eighty-six of 173 regimental commanders were killed or wounded.[1] Most of the wounded officers and enlisted men, as well as the stragglers, eventually returned to the army. But Lee would be unable to think about resuming his preferred strategy — the offensive — for another eight months.

The Confederate commander did not give up easily. "My Chief was most anxious to recross into Maryland" to salvage the campaign, wrote Lee's adjutant Walter Taylor on September 28. But in view of his army's condition, Lee changed his mind. "I would not hesitate to make [the attempt] even with our diminished numbers," he informed Jefferson Davis on September 25, "did the army exhibit its former temper and condition," but "the hazard would be great and a reverse disastrous. I am, therefore, led to pause."[2]

The army indeed did not exhibit its former temper for some time after Antietam. "I fear this Md. trip has rather injured us more than good done," wrote a Georgia captain on September 23. "Wee lost more than we gained in it, I think." A Georgia private whose regiment was badly cut up wrote home that "it looks like they are going to kill all the men in battle before they stop. This war will have to stop before long, as all the men will be killed off."[3] Some soldiers took out their frustrations by damning Marylanders. "Don't let any of your friends sing 'My Maryland,' not 'my West [er]n Md.' anyhow," wrote Walter Taylor to his sister. When a Confederate band struck up the song after the retreat to Virginia, it "was prevented by the groans and hisses of the soldiers."[4]

The battle and the Confederate retreat did great things for morale in the Army of the Potomac — even though some soldiers wondered why McClellan had not renewed the attack before the crippled rebels could escape. Nevertheless, "their retreat shows

Lutheran Church in Sharpsburg four days after the battle. This church was badly damaged by shell fire and later had to be torn down. At the time of this Alexander Gardner photograph, the church was being used as a Union field hospital. Several other buildings in the village (population 1,300 at the time of the battle) suffered similar damage. (National Archives)

how complete our victory was," wrote General John Gibbon, commander of the Iron Brigade, which had fought so savagely in the Cornfield. "We have whipped and dispirited them terribly," boasted a New York lieutenant. General Alpheus Williams, who had taken command of XII Corps after Mansfield was mortally wounded, wrote that "our men fought gloriously and we taught the rascals a lesson, which they much needed after Pope's disaster."[5]

General Orlando Willcox had taken over a IX Corps division after its commander was killed at Chantilly. "It was completely run down after a long series of what in fact amounted to disasters," Willcox wrote two weeks after Antietam, "but the late fights & all our efforts have brought it up wonderfully." A month after the battle a Maine soldier reported that "a different spirit has been infused into the hearts of the men. . . . Instead of faultfinding and repining which was once so general amongst the soldiers now is found contentment and cheerfulness and a right idea of the work before them."[6]

The Northern press broke out in a paroxysm of exultation, all the more exuberant because of the pessimism that had preceded it. "At no time since the war commenced did the cause of the Union look more dark and despairing than one week ago," declared the *New York Sunday Mercury* on September 21, but now "at no time since the first gun was fired have the hopes of the nation seemed in such a fair way of realization as they do today." It was too bad the rebels got away without further damage, "but when we recollect what a transition has taken place, from the depth of despondency to the height of exultation, from defeat to glorious victory, we ought to rejoice over what has been done, rather than grumble because we have not accomplished everything." The *New York Times* could scarcely find strong enough adjectives or big enough type to describe this "GREAT VICTORY" which "must take its place among the grand decisive conflicts of history. . . . Its effects will be seen and felt in the destinies of the Nation for centuries to come."[7]

The *Times* and other newspapers admitted that the surrender of Harpers Ferry was "humiliating . . . the most disgraceful thing of the war." And Lee's escape across the Potomac "will be a disappointment to the public at large."[8] But these events paled in comparison with the "glorious victory" at Antietam, which "raised the country from the darkest despondency" to "hope and elation." It "destroys the prestige of rebel invincibility . . . it restores confidence, solidity, and enthusiasm to our own troops" and has produced "the greatest damage [that] has been inflicted on the rebel cause . . . since the war began."[9] *Harper's Weekly* summed up the Northern public's perception of Antietam: the rebels had invaded Maryland "exultant, hopeful, flushed with triumph; they retire defeated, disappointed, disheartened."[10]

The initial Southern response to the news of Antietam — news that came first from Northern newspapers because there was no telegraph link from Lee's army to the South — was shock and disbelief. "It looks rather gloomy for our prospects in Md. and I cannot possibly understand it all," wrote a young Virginia woman when she learned of Lee's retreat. In Georgia, Lieutenant Charles C. Jones Jr. expressed "painful anxiety" about the fate of Lee's army.[11] The Richmond press implicitly acknowledged the nasty blow of news from Maryland when it denounced the "sheer and shameless fabrication . . . monstrous fables . . . nauseating absurdities" of Northern claims of Antietam as a victory. "It is strange that our community should have been so much excited by the lying reports of the Yankee papers," declared the *Richmond Dispatch*. There was no reason "for discouragement," for "Gen. Lee obtained a decided advantage" in the battle and then withdrew "perfectly at his leisure."[12]

The *Dispatch* and the *Enquirer* convinced themselves that the capture of Harpers Ferry was Lee's real objective and that the army's campaign of two weeks in Maryland was "among the most brilliant" in history. "Our people are disappointed because we did not gain a victory [at Sharpsburg] as decisive as those around Richmond and at Manassas." But "they cannot expect such victories always."[13] Addressing all those Southerners who "are not obstinately determined to be miserable" because of the lying reports of a great Union victory, the *Dispatch* asked on September 30: "If we have been thus badly beaten, why is no use made of the victory? Why has McClellan not crossed the river and destroyed the army of Gen. Lee? Why has the latter been allowed to refresh and recruit at his leisure? The truth is this: The victory, though not so decisive as that of Manassas, was certainly a Confederate victory." Lee's retreat, added the *Enquirer*, was merely a strategic maneuver, "like the crouch before the spring of the lion."[14]

Was all of this brave rhetoric another example of whistling past the graveyard? Perhaps so, but many of these themes became orthodoxy in the South during the weeks after the battle: Lee fought

McClellan to a standstill at Sharpsburg; his unmolested withdrawal and the repulse of McClellan's feeble pursuit were a thumb in the Yankees' eye; the capture of 12,000 Federals at Harpers Ferry was a major achievement; and therefore "the net result of the campaign was in our favor."[15]

This perception became even stronger after two Confederate offensives in the West came to grief in October. A small Union army commanded by William S. Rosecrans turned back a Confederate effort to recapture Corinth, Mississippi, in a vicious two-day battle October 3–4. Even the Southern press conceded that this affair was a defeat and "disaster."[16] And after a drawn battle at Perryville, Kentucky, on October 8, Braxton Bragg and Edmund Kirby Smith gave up their campaign and retreated again to Tennessee. These "two reverses" were serious but "by no means decisive," declared the Dispatch, because they were "counterbalanced" by the successes in Virginia including the capture of Harpers Ferry. "Instead, therefore, of desponding, we see cause to entertain the brightest hopes."[17] (See map insets, p. 136.)

This editorial was a tacit acknowledgment that many Southerners were indeed "desponding." That category included Jefferson Davis, who was "very low down after the battle of Sharpsburg," according to the Confederate secretary of war. Combined with the failure of the Kentucky invasion, the retreat from Maryland and the heavy losses of Lee's army especially in officers meant, said Davis, that the South's "maximum strength has been mobilized, while the enemy is just beginning to put forth his might."[18]

Northerners came up with an assorted mix of metaphors to celebrate the trinity of triumphs at Antietam, Corinth, and Perryville, of which Antietam was the greatest. "The wheel of fortune has turned around once more," wrote a diarist two days after that battle. There are "gleams of light that promise the return of sunshine," added another three weeks later.[19] Looking back over the three weeks that began with the battles at South Mountain on September 14, the *New York Herald* announced that "the battle of Antietam has broken the back of the rebellion" and "changed the tide of affairs, and victory now attends us everywhere."[20]

On September 13 President Lincoln had taken an hour out of his crisis schedule to meet with a delegation of Chicago clergymen bearing a petition urging a proclamation of emancipation. Lincoln did not tell them that a draft of such a proclamation had rested in a desk drawer for almost two months while he waited for the military situation to improve. That situation had instead gotten worse — and never more so than at that moment when Lee was in Maryland, McClellan had not confronted him yet, panic reigned in much of the North, and the war seemed on the verge of being lost. Lincoln's private secretary John Hay recalled this period as one of "fearful anxiety" and "almost unendurable tension" for the president.[21]

Some of that tension spilled over into his remarks to the delegation, which had claimed that emancipation was the will of God. "If it is probable that God would reveal his will to others, on a point so connected with my duty," said Lincoln testily, "it might be supposed he would reveal it directly to me." In present circumstances, with Rebel armies in Maryland and Kentucky and threatening Pennsylvania and Ohio, "what *good* would a proclamation of emancipation from me do . . . when I cannot even enforce the Constitution in the rebel States? . . . I don't want to issue a document the whole world will see must necessarily be inoperative, like the Pope's bull against the comet!"[22]

A week later all had changed. Five days after Antietam Lincoln called a special meeting of the Cabinet. He reminded members of their decision two months earlier to postpone issuance of an emancipation proclamation. "I think the time has come now," the president continued. "I wish it was a better time. . . . The action of the army against the rebels has not been quite what I should have best liked. But they have been driven out of Maryland." When the enemy was at Frederick, Lincoln had made a "promise to myself and (hesitating a little) to my Maker" that "if God gave us the victory in the approaching battle, [I] would consider it an indication of Divine will" in favor of emancipation. Perhaps recalling his conversation with the Chicago clergymen, Lincoln suggested that Antietam was God's sign that "he had decided this question in favor of the slaves." Therefore, said the president, he intended that day to issue the proclamation warning Confederate states that unless they returned to the Union by January 1, 1863, their slaves "shall be then, thenceforward, and forever free."[23]

Perhaps no consequence of Antietam

was more momentous than this one. It changed the character of the war, as General-in-Chief Halleck noted in a communication to Ulysses S. Grant: "There is now no possible hope of reconciliation. . . . We must conquer the rebels or be conquered by them. . . . Every slave withdrawn from the enemy is the equivalent of a white man put *hors de combat.*"[24] The proclamation would apply only to states in rebellion, which produced some confusion because it thus seemed to "liberate" those slaves who were mostly beyond Union authority while leaving in bondage those in the border states. This apparent anomaly caused disappointment among some abolitionists and radical Republicans. But most of them recognized that the commander in chief's legal powers extended only to *enemy* property. Some of that "property," however, *would* be freed by the Proclamation or by the practical forces of war because thousands of contrabands in Confederate states were already within Union lines.

And in any event, the symbolic power of the Proclamation changed the war from one to restore the Union into one to destroy the old Union and build a new one purged of human bondage. "GOD BLESS ABRAHAM LINCOLN!" blazoned Horace

Greeley's *New York Tribune* on September 23. "It is the beginning of the end of the rebellion; the beginning of the new life of the nation." The Emancipation Proclamation "is one of those stupendous facts in human history which marks not only an era in the progress of the nation, but an epoch in the history of the world." Speaking for African Americans, Frederick Douglass declared: "We shout for joy that we live to record this righteous decree."[25]

Democrats almost unanimously denounced the Proclamation and vowed to campaign against it in the fall congressional elections. Many border-state Unionists also complained loudly. Lincoln had already discounted this opposition, which had once concerned him so greatly. He had tried in vain to get the border states to move voluntarily, but now "we must make the forward movement" without them, he told the Cabinet. "They [will] acquiesce, if not immediately, soon." As for the Democrats, "their clubs would be used against us take what course we might."[26]

More serious, perhaps, was the potential for opposition in the army, especially by McClellanite officers in the Army of the Potomac. There was good reason for worry about this. General Fitz-John Porter branded Lincoln's document "the absurd proclamation of a political coward." It has "caused disgust, and expressions of disloyalty, to the views of the administration" in the army, wrote Porter privately.[27] McClellan himself considered the Proclamation "infamous" and told his wife that he could not "make up my mind to fight for such an accursed doctrine as that of a servile insurrection." McClellan consulted Democratic friends in New York, who advised him "to submit to the Presdt's proclamation & quietly continue doing my duty as a soldier." He even took action to quiet loose talk among some of his subordinates about marching on Washington to overthrow the government. On October 7 McClellan issued a general order reminding the army of its duty of obedience to civil authority. "The remedy for political errors, if any are committed," he noted in a none-too-subtle reference to the forthcoming elections, "is to be found in the action of the people at the polls."[28]

The issue of emancipation would continue — at times dangerously — to divide the army and the Northern public for another six months or more. But in the end, as the *Springfield* (Mass.) *Republican* predicted on September 24, 1862, it would "be sustained by the great mass of the loyal people." These were the people who agreed with Lincoln's words in his message to Congress on December 1, 1862: "Without slavery the rebellion could never have existed; without slavery it could not continue." The *Springfield Republican* proved to be right when it anticipated that "by the courage and prudence of the President, the greatest social and political revolution of the age will be triumphantly carried through in the midst of a civil war."[29]

The battle of Antietam and the Emancipation Proclamation had a signal impact abroad. Only two days before the first news of Antietam arrived in London, the Earl of Shaftesbury, Prime Minister Palmerston's son-in-law, told Confederate envoys John Slidell and James Mason that "the event you so strongly desire," a British–French offer of mediation and diplomatic recognition, "is very close at hand." But the news of Union victories in Maryland came as "a bitter draught and a stunning blow" to friends of the Confederacy in Britain, wrote the secretary of the American legation. "They express as much chagrin as if they themselves had been defeated."[30]

The London *Times* certainly was stunned by the "exceedingly remarkable" outcome of Antietam. "An army demoralized by a succession of failures," in the words of a *Times* editorial, "has suddenly proved at least equal, and we may probably say superior, to an army elated with triumph and bent upon a continuation of its conquests." Calling Lee's invasion of Maryland "a failure," the normally pro-Southern *Times* admitted that "the Confederates have suffered their first important check exactly at the period when they might have been thought most assured of victory."[31] Other British newspapers expressed similar sentiments. South Mountain and Antietam restored "our drooping credit here," reported American Minister Charles Francis Adams. Most Englishmen had expected the Confederates to capture Washington, and "the surprise" at their retreat "has been quite in proportion. . . . As a consequence, less and less appears to be thought of mediation and intervention."[32]

Adams's prognosis was correct. Prime Minister Palmerston now backed away from the idea of intervention. The only favorable condition for mediation "would be the great success of the South against the North," he pointed out to Foreign Secretary Russell on October 2. "That state of things seemed ten days ago to be approaching," but with Antietam "its advance has been lately checked." Thus "the whole matter is full of difficulty," and nothing could be done until the situation became more clear. By October 22 it was clear to Palmerston that Confederate defeats had ended any chance for successful mediation. "I am therefore inclined to change the opinion I wrote you when the Confederates seemed to be carrying all before them, and I am [convinced] . . . that we must continue merely to be lookers-on till the war shall have taken a more decided turn."[33]

Russell and Gladstone, plus Napoleon of France, did not give up easily. The French asked Britain to join in a proposal for a six-months' armistice in the American war during which the blockade would be lifted, cotton exports would be renewed, and peace negotiations would begin. France also approached Russia, which refused to take part in such an obviously pro-Confederate scheme. On November 12 the British Cabinet also rejected it after two days of discussions in which Secretary for War Sir George Cornewall Lewis led the opposition to intervention. In a letter six days later to King Leopold of Belgium, who favored the Confederacy and supported intervention, Palmerston explained the reasons for Britain's refusal to act. "Some months ago" when "the Confederates were gaining ground to the North of Washington, and events seemed to be in their favor," an "opportunity for making some communication" appeared imminent. But "the tide of war changed its course and the opportunity did not arrive."[34]

Most disappointed of all by this outcome was James Mason, who was left cooling his heels by the British refusal to recognize his own diplomatic status as well as that of his government. On the eve of the arrival in London of news about Antietam, Mason had been "much cheered and elated" by initial reports of Lee's invasion. "Recognition is not far off," he had written on October 1st. Dashed hopes soured Mason on the "obdurate" British, and he felt "that I should terminate the mission here."[35] He decided to stay on, but never again did his mission come so close to success as in September 1862.

The preliminary Emancipation Proclamation further eroded the Confederacy's chances for diplomatic recognition — though at first it seemed to have the contrary effect. The American minister to France warned Seward to expect "the most mischievous efforts" by Confederate sympathizers "to pervert and misconstrue the motives which have prompted the proclamation."[36] Anti-American conservatives in Britain and France, and even some liberals, professed to see the Proclamation not as a genuine antislavery act but as a cynical attempt to deflect European opinion or as a desperate effort to encourage a slave insurrection. If Lincoln really wanted to free the slaves, they asked, why did he announce that the Proclamation would apply to states where he had no power and exempt those where he did? The Proclamation was "cold, vindictive, and entirely political," wrote the British chargé d'affaires in Washington. Lord Russell, who had earlier censured the Lincoln administration for *not* acting against slavery, now perversely pronounced the preliminary Proclamation a vile encouragement to "acts of plunder, of incendiarism, and of revenge."[37]

The "incitement to insurrection" theme was based on a phrase in Lincoln's preliminary Proclamation stating that the govern-

This cartoon in the satirical British weekly *Punch* reflected the initial reaction by English conservatives to the Preliminary Emancipation Proclamation, which is portrayed as Lincoln's last desperate card in the deadly game against the Confederacy — the ace of spades with its malevolent black face, implying that the Proclamation was an attempt to set off the gunpowder of a slave insurrection. (*Punch*)

ment "will do no act or acts to repress" slaves "in any acts they may make for their actual freedom."[38] Lincoln, of course, meant that the army would not return slaves coming into Union lines. But the anti-American press (which included most major newspapers in Britain) seized upon this phrase as an excuse to berate Lincoln and the Union cause.

The *London Times* was the most notorious in this regard, seeing it as an opportunity to reopen the issue of British intervention on humanitarian grounds. With this Proclamation, declared the *Times*, Lincoln "will appeal to the black blood of the African; he will whisper of the pleasures of spoil and of the gratification of yet fiercer instincts; and when the blood begins to flow and shrieks come piercing through the darkness, Mr. LINCOLN will wait till the rising flames tell that all is consummated, and then he will rub his hands and think that revenge is sweet."[39] Many other British newspapers took their cue from the *Times*, branding the Proclamation "the last resort of a bewildered statesman," "the wretched makeshift of a pettifogging lawyer," "the last arm of vengeance . . . to carry the war of the knife to private homes where women and children are left undefended."[40]

British friends of the Union understood this "demoniacal cry" by "the ghouls of the English press" for what it was.[41] "In England," wrote John Stuart Mill to an American friend, "the proclamation has only increased the venom of those who after taunting you for so long with caring nothing for abolition, now reproach you for your abolitionism as the worst of your crimes." But these "wretched effusions," said Mill, came from conservatives "who so hate your democratic institutions that they would be sure to inveigh against you whatever you did, and are enraged at no longer being able to taunt you with being false to your own principles." Benjamin Moran, the acidulous secretary of the American legation, wrote that the response of the British press to the Proclamation exposed "the hollowness of the anti-slavery professions of this people. . . . Altho' they know that Mr. Lincoln is in earnest, they so desire us to be crushed that they won't believe him."[42]

But the "effusions" of the anti-American press probably did not reflect the sentiments of a majority of the British people. And this majority was not silent. The *London Morning Star* spoke for them when it pronounced the Proclamation "a gigantic stride in the paths of Christian and civilized progress — the turning point in the history of the American commonwealth — an act only second in courage and probable results to the Declaration of Independence."[43] In November 1862, pro-Union forces in Britain began to organize meetings and circulate petitions in favor of the Proclamation. When Lincoln on January 1st confounded European cynics who had predicted that he would never issue the final Proclamation, pro-Union sentiments in Britain grew stronger. Lincoln implicitly responded to criticisms of the preliminary Proclamation by stating in the final version that emancipation was "an act of justice" as well as a military measure, and by enjoining freed slaves to refrain from violence.[44]

Even though the final Proclamation exempted states or parts of states containing one-quarter of all slaves, it nevertheless announced a new war aim that foreshadowed universal emancipation if the North won the war. A black Methodist clergyman in Washington, Henry M. Turner, rejoiced that "the time has come in the history of this nation, when the downtrodden and abject black man can assert his rights, and feel his manhood. . . . The first day of January, 1863, is destined to form one of the most memorable epochs in the history of the world."[45]

As recognition of this truth dawned across the Atlantic, huge mass meetings in Britain adopted pro-Union resolutions and sent copies to the American legation — some fifty of them in all.[46] "The Emancipation Proclamation has done more for us here than all our former victories and all our diplomacy," wrote Henry Adams from London on January 23. "It is creating an almost convulsive reaction in our favor all over this country." The largest of the meetings, at Exeter Hall in London, "has had a powerful effect on our newspapers and politicians," wrote Richard Cobden, one of the foremost pro-Union members of Parliament. "It has closed the mouths of those who have been advocating the side of the South. Recognition of the South, by England, whilst it bases itself on Negro slavery, is an impossibility." Similar reports came from elsewhere in Europe. "The anti-slavery position of the government is at length giving us a substantial foothold in European circles," wrote the American minister to the Netherlands. "Everyone can understand the significance of a war where emancipation is written on one banner and slavery on the other."[47]

Antietam and emancipation had important consequences for American politics at home as well as diplomacy abroad. The state and congressional elections of 1862 in the North loomed as potential obstacles to the administration's ability to maintain home-front support for its war policies. The two policies that became the main Democratic targets were "arbitrary arrests" and emancipation.

On September 24, two days after the preliminary Emancipation Proclamation, Lincoln issued a second edict suspending the writ of *habeas corpus* and authorizing military trials for "all Rebels and Insurgents, their aiders and abettors within the United States, and all persons discouraging volunteer enlistments, resisting militia drafts, or guilty of any disloyal practice."[48] This order was aimed primarily at those who resisted by riots or shootings the enforcement of the draft for nine-months' militia authorized by Congress in July. Although most areas raised their militia quotas by volunteering, and opposition to the draft in remaining areas was largely peaceful, intense violence did break out in a few localities. Espionage and guerrilla activities also remained a serious problem in border states, especially during the Confederate invasions of Maryland and Kentucky. The Constitution authorized suspension of the writ of *habeas corpus* in time of rebellion or invasion (Article I, Section 9). During the war as a whole the Lincoln administration used this power sparingly in the free states. But arrests escalated during the tense period of August and September 1862, giving Democrats an opportunity to make political capital out of the government's alleged violations of civil liberties.[49]

More important as a Democratic issue in 1862, however, was emancipation. Denouncing the Emancipation Proclamation as unconstitutional, Democrats also appealed to the racial fears and prejudices of many Northern voters. In state and district party conventions, Democratic resolutions denounced the Black Republican "party of fanaticism" that intended to free "two or three million semi-savages" to "overrun the North and enter into competition with the white laboring masses" and mix with "their sons and daughters." Midwestern Democratic orators proclaimed that "every white man in the North, who does not want to be swapped off for a free Nigger, should vote the Democratic ticket."[50]

The most important state election would take place in New York, where the Democrats nominated for governor Horatio Seymour, a veteran of thirty years in state politics who had served a previous term as governor. "A vote for Seymour," declared the leading Democratic newspaper in New

York, the *World*, "is a vote to protect our white laborers against the association and competition of Southern negroes." Seymour himself denounced emancipation as "a proposal for the butchery of women and children, for scenes of lust and rapine, and of arson and murder."[51]

But the issue of these Northern elections that subsumed all others was the war itself. On this question the Democrats sent forth a mixed and uncertain message. Peace Democrats, especially in the Midwest, made no secret of their opposition to the war as a means to restore the Union. War Democrats like Seymour and Manton Marble, editor of the *World*, endorsed restoration of the Union "as it was" by military victory and attacked the Lincoln administration for its failure to achieve that victory. Republicans responded with charges that War Democrats were no better than Copperheads. One of the mildest of such accusations was a *New York Times* editorial which maintained that Seymour's "thin disguise of loyalty" merely cloaked a "formidable attempt to cripple the National Administration in the very midst of its contest with the rebellion."[52]

Republicans of course exaggerated the disloyalty of Democrats for political effect.

But they did not make up their charges out of whole cloth. Even such a temperate, impartial observer as Lord John Lyons, British minister to the United States, was convinced after speaking with War Democrats in New York that they desired "to put an end to the war even at the risk of losing the Southern States altogether." If Democrats won control of the House, reported Lyons, they expected Lincoln to read the handwriting on the wall and "endeavor to effect a reconciliation with the people of the South."[53]

Whatever the accuracy of Lyons' observation, there is no doubt of the truth of Republican claims that a Democratic victory in 1862 "will be interpreted in Secessia and Europe as a vote for stopping the war."[54] The correspondence of European diplomats favoring a mediation offer explicitly stated such an assumption. Southerners interpreted Democratic gains in the states that held their elections in October — Pennsylvania, Ohio, and Indiana — as a "matter of more serious interest than the military news," for they indicated that "Lincoln and the Republicans are about to be overthrown" by Northern voters who expressed a "willingness for peace."[55]

Before Antietam, Republicans and Democrats alike considered the prospect of Democratic control of the House all but certain. The Democrats nominated their candidates and adopted their "war is a failure" platforms during those August and early September days of "profound despondency," noted the New York Times in October. "Thousands, whose hearts were depressed by the reverses of the war, were ready for the moment to seek a remedy in any quarter." But now "our armies have achieved brilliant victories" that reinvigorated Northern determination to see the war through to victory.[56]

The election of 1862 in Maine, a rock-ribbed Republican state, confirmed the Times's analysis of pre-Antietam sentiments. Maine held its election in early September. The Republican candidate for governor won with 53 percent of the vote, but this was a significant decline from the 62 percent the Republicans had gotten in 1860. If they were to suffer that kind of proportionate decline in other states (most of them more evenly contested than Maine), the Republicans would indeed lose the House in 1862.[57]

If the elections had been held any time during the three weeks after Antietam, however, Republicans might have defied the tradition of significant losses by the party in power in mid-term elections and retained their two-to-one majority in the House. (In every mid-term election for the previous twenty years the opposition party had actually *won* control of the House.) But the post-Antietam euphoria — and its attendant political benefits — gradually wore off during those three weeks. The main reason was the inactivity of the Army of the Potomac. McClellan had not only failed to renew the attack on September 18; he also sat tight on the north side of the Potomac for almost six weeks while he reorganized and resupplied the army. But that gave Lee time to reorganize and resupply *his* army, which needed the time much more than the Federals.

As day after day of fine fall weather passed, frustration with McClellan's failure to move grew stronger. "Will the Army of the Potomac Advance?" asked headlines in Northern newspapers. "Why Should There be Delay?"[58] "What devil is it that prevents the Potomac Army from moving?" asked the *Chicago Tribune* on October 13. "What malign influence palsies our army and wastes these glorious days for fighting?"

On October 10–12 Jeb Stuart again thumbed his nose at the Yankees and then stuck the thumb in their eyes by riding around McClellan's whole army with impunity. Stuart's 1,800 troopers raided as far north as Chambersburg, Pennsylvania, evaded the Union cavalry that tried to intercept them, and returned to their own lines bringing 1,200 captured horses and dozens of prisoners with the loss of only two men. Gideon Welles was far from the only person to lament this "humiliating, disgraceful" fiasco, which was more evidence of McClellan's "inertness, and imbecility. . . . The country groans, but nothing is done. Certainly the confidence of the people must give way under this fatuous inaction."[59]

Democrats made significant gains in the Pennsylvania congressional elections on October 13, one day after the completion of Stuart's raid. This was no coincidence. Voters took out their anger by voting against the party in power. Republicans were frustrated by the irony, in the *New York Tribune*'s words, "that Republican candidates should lose because Democratic Generals won't fight." Lincoln undoubtedly shared this sentiment. But he also accepted the political reality that the commander in chief takes the blame for failure just as he benefits from success. "With the administration military success is everything," observed an astute Boston Republican; "it is the verdict which cures all errors."[60]

Lincoln did everything he could to prod McClellan into action. The president had visited the Army of the Potomac on October 1–4 and had personally told McClellan to get moving. After returning to Washington, Lincoln had Halleck send McClellan an order that any other general would have considered peremptory: "Cross the Potomac and give battle to the enemy. . . . Your army must move now while the roads are good." Nothing happened — except Stuart's raid. Lincoln reined in his anger about that misadventure for almost two weeks before bursting out with a telegram to McClellan in reply to an excuse from the general about broken-down horses: "Will you pardon me for asking what the horses of your army have done since the battle of Antietam that fatigues anything?"[61]

More temperately, the president wrote McClellan a fatherly letter. "You remember my speaking to you of what I called your over-cautiousness," Lincoln

General McClellan and President Lincoln plus various officers at V Corps headquarters near the Antietam battlefield on October 3, 1862, where Lincoln vainly urged McClellan to follow up his victory with a vigorous pursuit of the enemy. (Library of Congress)

reminded him. "Are you not over-cautious when you assume that you can not do what the enemy is constantly doing?" McClellan had insisted that his men could not march and fight without full rations and new shoes. Yet the enemy marched and fought with scanty rations and few shoes. To wait for a full supply pipeline "ignores the question of *time*," which benefited the enemy more than it did Union forces. If McClellan crossed the Potomac quickly and got between the enemy and Richmond, said Lincoln, he could force Lee into the open for a decisive battle. "We should not so operate as to merely drive him away," maintained the president. "If we can not beat the enemy where he now is [west of Harpers Ferry], we never can. . . . If we never try, we shall never succeed."[62]

But McClellan still delayed. Halleck threw up his hands in exasperation. "I am sick, tired, and disgusted," he said. "There is an immobility here that exceeds all that any man can conceive of. It requires the lever of Archimedes to move this inert mass."[63] On October 26 the Army of the Potomac finally began to cross its namesake river. But it took six days to get the whole army across (the Army of Northern Virginia had done it in one night after Antietam) and another seven days to move fifty miles to the vicinity of Warrenton. Lee divided his smaller force again and placed Longstreet's corps between the enemy and Richmond. Jackson stayed in the Valley on McClellan's flank, confident that he could outmarch the Yankees to join Longstreet if necessary.

For Lincoln this was the last straw. Tired of trying to "bore with an auger too dull to take hold," he relieved McClellan and ordered Burnside to take command of the army on November 7. To his private secretary Lincoln later explained this decision: "I peremptorily ordered him to advance," but McClellan kept "delaying on little pretexts of wanting this and that. I began to fear he was playing false — that he did not want to hurt the enemy. I saw how he could intercept the enemy on the way to Richmond. I determined to make that the test. If he let them get away I would remove him. He did so & I relieved him."[64]

Nothing in McClellan's tenure of command became him like the leaving of it. Despite emotional pleas from some officers and men to defy Lincoln's order and "change front on Washington," McClellan discountenanced all such talk and turned the army over to a reluctant Burnside. "Stand by General Burnside as you have stood by me, and all will be well," he told his soldiers as thousands yelled their continuing affection for him and others wept unashamedly. McClellan boarded a train for New Jersey, where he would sit out the rest of the war except for a run against Lincoln as the Democratic candidate for president in 1864. In that effort, as a Union naval officer wryly put it, he met "with no better success as a politician than as a general."[65]

McClellan's farewell to the Army of the Potomac on November 10, 1862 (detail). (*Harper's Weekly*)

Lincoln had waited until after the elections to remove McClellan. Those elections resulted in significant Democratic gains: the governorship of New York; the governorship and a legislative majority in New Jersey; legislative majorities in Illinois and Indiana; and a net increase of thirty-four members of the U.S. House of Representatives. If gubernatorial elections had been held in Pennsylvania, Ohio, Illinois, and Indiana in 1862, Democrats might have won them also. Contemporaries and most historians have interpreted these elections as "a great, sweeping revolution of public sentiment," "a near disaster for the Republicans," "a great triumph for the Democrats."[66]

In reality they were nothing of the sort. Republicans retained the governorships of all but two of the eighteen Northern states and the legislatures of all but three. They made an unprecedented gain of five seats in the Senate. And they kept a majority of twenty-five in the House after experiencing the smallest net loss of House seats in twenty years — indeed, the only time in those two decades that the party in power retained control of the House.[67]

What might have happened without Antietam could well have been a different story. A shift of an average of 1 percent of the votes to Democrats in sixteen Republican-held congressional districts in nine states would have given Democrats a comfortable majority in the House.[68] And who can doubt that a Confederate victory at Antietam and/or the continued presence of the Army of Northern Virginia in Maryland or Pennsylvania would have swayed that tiny percentage of voters — and more. That would indeed have been a disaster for Republicans and a great triumph for Democrats — especially the Peace Democrats.

It might also have meant disaster for the Union cause.

To the end of his life McClellan believed that Antietam was his finest hour, when he had saved the Union and earned the gratitude of the republic. Perhaps he was right. Several pivotal moments occurred in the Civil War. McClellan was involved in two of them. As his splendidly trained and equipped Army of the Potomac advanced up the Virginia Peninsula in May 1862, the Confederacy was on the ropes. Much of its South Atlantic coast was gone. New Orleans, Nashville, and several other cities had fallen. Union forces had gained control of most of the crucial Cumberland–Tennessee–Mississippi River network. Twenty-five thousand Southern soldiers had become prisoners of war. The government was preparing to flee Richmond. One more punch by McClellan might have knocked the Confederacy out of the war. But McClellan could not bring himself to throw that punch.

Instead, Stonewall Jackson and Robert E. Lee got the South off the mat at the count of nine and began counterpunching with such skill and power that by September the Union appeared to be on the ropes. This remarkable turnaround was the war's first pivotal moment. Now it was Washington that seemed to be in danger. Confederate armies marched into Maryland and Kentucky in a campaign to win these states and conquer a peace. Foreign nations were preparing to recognize Confederate independence. Northern armies and voters were demoralized. Lincoln had shelved his proposed edict of emancipation to wait for a victory that might never come. But it did, along the ridges and in the woods and cornfields between Antietam Creek and the Potomac River in the single bloodiest day in all of American history.

The victory at Antietam could have been more decisive. The same was true of two lesser victories that followed at Corinth and Perryville. But Union armies had stymied the supreme Confederate efforts. Foreign powers backed away from intervention and recognition, and never again came so close to considering them. Lincoln issued his Emancipation Proclamation. Northern voters chastised but did not overthrow the Republican party, which forged ahead with its program to preserve the Union and give it a new birth of freedom. Here indeed was a pivotal moment.

No other campaign and battle in the war had such momentous, multiple consequences as Antietam. In July 1863 the dual Union triumphs at Gettysburg and Vicksburg struck another blow that blunted a renewed Confederate offensive in the East and cut off the western third of the Confederacy from the rest. In September 1864 Sherman's capture of Atlanta reversed another decline in Northern morale and set the stage for the final drive to Union victory. These also were pivotal moments. But they would never have happened if the triple Confederate offensives in Mississippi, Kentucky, and most of all Maryland had not been defeated in the fall of 1862.

Contemporaries recognized Antietam as the preeminent turning point of the war. Jefferson Davis was depressed by the outcome there because the Confederacy had put forth its maximum effort and failed. Two of the war's best corps commanders, who fought each other at Antietam (and several other battlefields), Winfield Scott Hancock for the Union and James Longstreet for the Confederacy, made the same point. In 1865 Hancock looked back on the past four years and concluded that "the battle of Antietam was the heaviest disappointment the rebels had met with. They then felt certain of success and felt that they should carry the war so far into the Northern states that the recognition of the Confederacy would have been a necessity." And twenty years after the war, Longstreet wrote simply: "At Sharpsburg was sprung the keystone of the arch upon which the Confederate cause rested."[69] Only with the collapse of that arch could the future of the United States as one nation, indivisible and free, be assured.

Notes

INTRODUCTION

1. The estimated number of those killed in the terrorist attacks of September 11, 2001, was 3,051 (*New York Times,* April 11, 2002; see also ibid., Oct. 25, Nov. 21, 2001). For casualty figures at Antietam, see note 56 for chapter 4 of this book. The 15,000 wounded survivors of Antietam, many of them crippled for life, were more than double the number of injured survivors of the attack on the World Trade Center and the Pentagon.

2. Tully McCrea to Belle McCrea, Sept. 20, 1862, in *Dear Belle: Letters from a Cadet & Officer to His Sweetheart, 1858–1865,* ed. Catherine S. Crary (Middletown, Conn., 1965), p. 155; George Breck's letter of September 18, published in the *Rochester Union and Advertiser,* Sept. 26, 1862, from the research notes of John Hennessy, used with permission.

3. Josiah Favill, *Diary of a Young Officer*

(Chicago, 1909), pp. 189–90; the diary of Otho Nesbitt, entry of Sept. 19, 1862, copy in the Antietam National Battlefield Library.

4. Nelson Miles to his brother, Sept. 24, 1862, copy in 61st New York file, and Diary of Ephraim E. Brown, entry of Sept. 19, 1862, in the 64th New York file, Antietam National Battlefield (these regiments were consolidated during the battle); Samuel Wheelock Fiske to *Springfield Republican*, Sept. 20, 1862, in *Mr. Dun Browne's Experiences in the Army*, ed. Stephen W. Sears (New York, 1998), p. 10.

5. Article by "D" in *Waterbury American*, Oct. 10, 1862, from the research notes of John Hennessy, used with permission.

6. *Hagerstown Herald*, Sept. 24, 1862, extract in the files of the Antietam National Battlefield Library; William Child to his wife, Sept. 22, 25, Oct. 19, 5th New Hampshire file, Antietam National Battlefield Library.

7. George K. Harlow to his family, June 3, 1863 (misdated; should be June 23), quoted in John M. Priest, *Antietam: The Soldiers' Battle* (Shippensburg, Pa., 1989), p. 316.

8. Rufus R. Dawes, *Service with the Sixth Wisconsin Volunteers* (Madison, 1890), p. 95; survey cited in Stephen W. Sears, *Landscape Turned Red: The Battle of Antietam* (New Haven, 1983), p. xii.
9. Private Henry J. Savage, in *Lee's Terrible Swift Sword: From Antietam to Chancellorsville: An Eyewitness History*, ed. Richard Wheeler (New York, 1992), p. 124.
10. Henry L. Abbott to his father, Nov. 20, 1862, in *Fallen Leaves: The Civil War Letters of Major Henry Livermore Abbott*, ed. Robert Garth Scott (Kent, Ohio, 1992), p. 143.
11. Quoted in Gary W. Gallagher, ed., *The Antietam Campaign* (Chapel Hill, 1999), pp. 47, 223.
12. William Child to his wife, Sept. 22, Oct. 19, 20, 1862, 5th New Hampshire file, Antietam National Battlefield Library.
13. Shaw to Francis G. Shaw, Sept. 21, 1862, in *Blue-Eyed Child of Fortune: The Civil War Letters of Robert Gould Shaw*, ed. Russell Duncan (Athens, Ga., 1992), p. 242.
14. *Die Presse* (Vienna), Oct. 12, 1862, translated and reprinted in *Karl Marx*

on *America and the Civil War*, ed. Saul
K. Padover (New York, 1972), p. 220;
Walter H. Taylor, Four Years with
General Lee, ed. James I. Robertson Jr.
(Bloomington, Ind., 1962), p. 67.

ONE
1. McClellan to Ellen Marcy McClellan,
   Aug. 9, 1861, McClellan Papers,
   Library of Congress.
2. Montgomery Blair to Francis P. Blair,
   Oct. 1, 1861, Blair–Lee Papers,
   Firestone Library, Princeton University.
3. George B. McClellan to Samuel L. M.
   Barlow, Nov. 8, 1861, Barlow Papers,
   the Huntington Library.
4. *The Collected Works of Abraham Lincoln*, ed. Roy P. Basler et al., 9 vols.
   (New Brunswick, N.J., 1953–1955), 5:
   95; "General M. C. Meigs on the
   Conduct of the Civil War," *American
   Historical Review* 26 (1921): 292.
5. *New York Times*, Feb. 8, 9, 11, 13, 17,
   1862.
6. *New York Tribune*, Feb. 13, 18, 1862.
7. *New York Herald*, Feb. 8, 12, 13, 24,
   March 12, 1862.
8. *Harper's Weekly*, March 1, 22, 1862.
9. Ibid., March 8, 1862.

10. *Richmond Enquirer,* Feb. 14, 1862; *Richmond Dispatch,* Feb. 17, March 17, 1862.
11. *Richmond Examiner,* Feb. 21, 1862; *Richmond Whig,* Feb. 22, 1862.
12. John B. Jones, *A Rebel War Clerk's Diary,* ed. Earl Schenck Miers (New York, 1958), pp. 67, 68, 69: diary entries of Feb. 20, 25, 27, 1862; *Inside the Confederate Government, The Diary of Robert Garlick Hill Kean,* ed. Edward Younger (New York, 1957), p. 23.
13. Stephens quoted in William C. Davis, *The Union That Shaped the Confederacy: Robert Toombs & Alexander Stephens* (Lawrence, Kansas, 2001), p. 191; Bragg quoted in Stephen W. Sears, *To the Gates of Richmond: The Peninsula Campaign* (New York, 1992), p. 12.
14. Hudson Strode, *Jefferson Davis: Confederate President* (New York, 1959), pp. 199, 201.
15. *The Diary of Dolly Lunt Burge,* ed. James I. Robertson Jr. (Athens, Ga., 1962), pp. 123, 124: entries of Feb. 10, 28, 1862; *"Journal of a Secesh Lady": The Diary of Catherine Ann Devereux Edmondston, 1860–1866,* ed. Beth G. Crabtree and James W. Patton (Raleigh, N.C., 1979), pp. 114, 115,

125: entries of Feb. 10, 11, 22, 1862.

16. *The Private Journal of Henry William Ravenel, 1859–1887*, ed. Arney Robinson Childs (Columbia, S.C., 1947), pp. 118, 129: entries of Feb. 19, March 18, 1862.

17. Mary Jones to Charles C. Jones Jr., Feb. 21, 1862, and Charles C. Jones Jr., to Mary Jones, March 18, 1862, in *Children of Pride: A True Story of Georgia and the Civil War*, ed. Robert Manson Mayers (New Haven, 1972), pp. 852, 863; James M. Griffin to Leila Griffin, Feb. 26, 1862, in *A Gentleman and an Officer: A Military and Social History of James B. Griffin's Civil War*, ed. Judith N. McArthur and Orville Vernon Burton (New York, 1996), pp. 163–65.

18. *Richmond Enquirer*, Feb. 28, 25, April 22, 1862; *Richmond Dispatch*, Feb. 13, 14, 1862.

19. John Geary to Mary Geary, April 16, 1862, in *A Politician Goes to War: The Civil War Letters of John White Geary*, ed. William Alan Blair (University Park, Pa., 1995), p. 41; *New York Times*, Feb. 25, 1862.

20. *War of the Rebellion . . . Official Records of the Union and Confederate Armies*,

128 vols. (Washington, 1880–1901), ser. 1, vol. 10, pt. 1, p. 384. Hereinafter abbreviated *O.R.*

21. Bruce Catton, *Grant Moves South* (Boston, 1960), p. 241.

22. *New York Times*, April 9, 1862; *Atlanta Confederacy*, reprinted in *New York Tribune*, April 30, 1862.

23. Bruce Catton, *Terrible Swift Sword* (New York, 1963), p. 261.

24. Elizabeth Blair Lee to Samuel Phillips Lee, May 7, 1862, in *Wartime Washington: The Civil War Letters of Elizabeth Blair Lee*, ed. Virginia Jeans Laas (Urbana, Ill., 1991), p. 139; *New York Herald*, April 30, 1862.

25. *New Orleans Delta*, April 26, 1862; *Norfolk Day Book*, April 29, 1862; *Raleigh State Journal*, May 3, 1862; *Richmond Enquirer*, April 29, 1862.

26. *Milledgeville Union*, reprinted in *Richmond Enquirer*, May 2, 1862; *Richmond Dispatch*, May 1, 1862.

27. *The Diary of Edmund Ruffin*, ed. William Kauffman Scarborough, 3 vols. (Baton Rouge, 1972–1989), 3: 291: entry of April 30, 1862; "*Journal of a Secesh Lady*," pp. 164–65: entry of April 28, 1862.

28. *Mary Chesnut's Civil War*, ed. C. Vann

Woodward (New Haven, 1981), p. 330: entry of April 27, 1862; Charles Minor Blackford to his wife, April 30, 1862, in *Letters from Lee's Army*, ed. Charles M. Blackford III (New York, 1947), p. 83.

29. *New York Tribune*, June 5, 1862; *Harper's Weekly*, June 21, 1862.
30. Lincoln to McClellan, April 10, 1862, *Collected Works of Lincoln*, 5: 185.
31. Stephen W. Sears, *George B. McClellan: The Young Napoleon* (New York, 1988), p. 165.
32. *New York Herald*, April 2, 1862.
33. Brewster to his mother, May 4, 1862, in *When This Cruel War Is Over: The Civil War Letters of Charles Harvey Brewster*, ed. David W. Blight (Amherst, Mass., 1992), p. 121; Francis A. Donaldson to Jacob Donaldson, May 25, 1862, in *Inside the Army of the Potomac: The Civil War Experience of Captain Francis Adams Donaldson*, ed. J. Gregory Acken (Mechanicsburg, Pa., 1998), p. 85; Kerry A. Trask, *Fire Within: A Civil War Narrative from Wisconsin* (Kent, Ohio, 1995), p. 111.
34. *New York Times*, May 9, 12, 1862; *New York Herald*, May 11, 1862.

35. Elizabeth Blair Lee to Samuel Phillips Lee, April 4, June 5, 1862, in Laas, *Wartime Washington*, pp. 123, 154; *Diary of a Union Lady, 1861–1865* (Maria Lydig Daly), ed. Harold Earl Hammond (New York, 1962), p. 127: entry of May 11, 1862.
36. *Richmond Enquirer*, May 3, 1862.
37. Jones, *Rebel War Clerk's Diary*, p. 75: entry of May 9, 1862; Cary Harrison quoted in James Marten, "A Feeling of Restless Anxiety," in *The Richmond Campaign of 1862*, ed. Gary W. Gallagher (Chapel Hill, N.C., 2000), p. 124.
38. Jones, *Rebel War Clerk's Diary*, p. 73: entry of April 18, 1862; Scarborough, *The Diary of Edmund Ruffin*, 3: 308: entry of May 19, 1862.
39. Helen Keary to her mother, May 7, 1862, in Edward A. Pollard, *Southern History of the War*, 2 vols. (New York, 1866), pp. 381–82n.
40. *The Journals of Josiah Gorgas, 1857–1878*, ed. Sarah Woolfolk Wiggins (Tuscaloosa, Ala., 1995), p. 45: entry of May 11, 1862.
41. Charles C. Jones Jr. to Charles C. Jones, May 12, *Children of Pride*, p. 893.

42. Ephraim Douglass Adams, *Great Britain and the American Civil War*, 2 vols. (New York, 1925), 1: 263.

43. Brian Jenkins, *Britain and the War for the Union*, 2 vols. (Montreal, 1974), 1: 104.

44. *Richmond Enquirer*, June 6, 18, 1862; Judah Benjamin to James Mason, April 12, July 19, 1862, in Virginia Mason, *The Public Life and Diplomatic Correspondence of James M. Mason* (New York, 1906), pp. 294, 303.

45. Lynn M. Case and Warren F. Spencer, *The United States and France: Civil War Diplomacy* (Philadelphia, 1970), p. 250; Charles M. Hubbard, *The Failure of Confederate Diplomacy* (Knoxville, 1998), p. xv; Howard Jones, *Union in Peril: The Crisis over British Intervention in the Civil War* (Chapel Hill, N.C., 1992), pp. 3, 10.

46. Quoted in Henry Donaldson Jordan and Edwin J. Pratt, *Europe and the American Civil War* (Boston, 1931), p. 17.

47. Henry Adams to Henry Raymond, Jan. 24, 1862, in *The Letters of Henry Adams: Vol. I, 1858–1868*, ed. J. C. Levenson (Cambridge, Mass., 1982), p. 272; *New York Tribune*, February 11, 1862.

48. James Mason to Robert M. T. Hunter, March 11, 1862, in *Public Life and Diplomatic Correspondence of Mason*, p. 266; Charles Francis Adams to William H. Seward, March 13, 1862, in *Papers Relating to the Foreign Affairs of the United States, 1862*, pt. 1 (Washington, 1863), p. 48; Henry Adams to Charles Francis Adams Jr., March 15, 1862, in *Letters of Henry Adams*, pp. 284–85.

49. *The Times*, March 31, 1862; William L. Dayton to William H. Seward, April 17, 1862, in *Papers Relating to Foreign Affairs, 1862*, pt. 1, p. 333.

50. Henry Adams to Charles Francis Adams Jr., May 16, *Letters of Henry Adams*, pp. 297–98; James Mason to Jefferson Davis, May 16, *Public Life and Diplomatic Correspondence of Mason*, p. 276.

51. James Mason to Lord John Russell, Aug. 2, 1862, and Russell to Mason, Aug. 2, in *Public Life and Diplomatic Correspondence of Mason*, pp. 327–29; Palmerston to Austen H. Layard, June 19, 1862, in Hubert Du Brulle, " 'A War of Wonders': The Battle in Britain over Americanization and the American Civil War" (Ph.D. diss.,

University of California at Santa Barbara, 1999), p. 210n.

52. Adams to Seward, June 26, March 13, 1862, *Papers Relating to Foreign Affairs, 1862*, pt. 1, pp. 118, 48.

TWO

1. *New York Herald*, May 26, 1862; *New York Times*, May 26, 27, 1862.
2. *Richmond Enquirer*, May 27, 1862.
3. William Nugent to Nellie Nugent, May 26, 1862, in *The Brothers' War: Civil War Letters to Their Loved Ones from the Blue and Gray*, ed. Annette Tapert (New York, 1988), p. 57; Charles C. Jones to Charles C. Jones Jr., May 28, 1862, in *Children of Pride: A True Story of Georgia and the Civil War*, ed. Robert Manson Myers (New Haven, 1972), p. 897.
4. Grace Brown Elmore, *Heritage of Woe: The Civil War Diary of Grace Brown Elmore, 1861–1868*, ed. Mark F. Weiner (Athens, Ga., 1997), diary entry of May 11, 1862, referring to Jackson's first victory, at McDowell, Virginia, on May 8.
5. George B. McClellan to Abraham Lincoln, April 20, 1862, in *The Civil War Papers of George B. McClellan:*

Selected Correspondence 1860–1865, ed. Stephen W. Sears (New York, 1989), pp. 244–45; Confederate officer quoted in Douglas Southall Freeman, *R. E. Lee: A Biography*, 4 vols. (New York, 1934–35), 2: 92.

6. *O.R.*, ser. 1, vol. 11, pt. 1, p. 61.

7. *Richmond Enquirer*, July 4, 1862; *Richmond Dispatch*, July 2, 1862.

8. Kate Stone, *Brokenburn: The Journal of Kate Stone, 1861–1868*, ed. John Q. Anderson (Baton Rouge, 1955), p. 129: diary entry of July 9, 1862; Charles C. Jones Jr. to parents, July 9, 1862, in Myers, ed., *Children of Pride*, p. 927; John B. Jones, *A Rebel War Clerk's Diary*, ed. Earl Schenck Miers (New York, 1958), p. 89: entry of July 9, 1862.

9. *New York Times*, July 3, 1862; *New York Herald*, July 3, 1862; *New York World*, July 7, 1862; *Chicago Tribune* quoted in Allan Nevins, *The War for the Union, Vol. 2: War Becomes Revolution* (New York, 1960), p. 140; *Illinois State Register* (Springfield), July 3, 1862.

10. *New York World*, July 4, 1862; Hannah Ropes to Alice Ropes, July 3, 1862, in *Civil War Nurse: The Diary and Letters*

of *Hannah Ropes*, ed. John R. Brumgardt (Knoxville, 1980), p. 50.

11. Adam Gurowski, *Diary from March 4, 1861 to November 12, 1862* (Boston, 1862; rep. New York, 1968), p. 235: entry of July 4, 1862; Lincoln quoted by Henry C. Deming, in *Recollected Words of Abraham Lincoln*, ed. Don E. Fehrenbacher and Virginia Fehrenbacher (Stanford, Calif., 1996), pp. 136–37.

12. Quoted in Louis M. Starr, *Reporting the Civil War: The Bohemian Brigade in Action, 1861–1865* (New York: Collier Books, 1962), p. 44.

13. *Harper's Weekly*, July 19, 1862.

14. *New York Times*, July 13, 23, Aug. 2, 1862; *New York Tribune*, July 15, 16, 1862.

15. *New York World*, July 9, 1862; *New York Times*, July 22, 1862.

16. Morse to Amos Kendall, July 23, 1862, in *Samuel F. B. Morse: His Letters and Journals*, ed. Edward L. Morse, 2 vols. (Boston, 1914), 2: 420; Charles Vail to John Vail, July 28, 1862, quoted in William Gillette, *Jersey Blue: Civil War Politics in New Jersey 1854–1865* (New Brunswick, N.J., 1995), p. 197.

17. *The Diary of George Templeton Strong,*

Vol. 3: The Civil War, 1860–1865, ed. Allan Nevins and Milton Halsey Thomas (New York, 1952), pp. 239, 241, 269: entries of July 11, 14, Aug. 4, 1862; *The Diary of Orville Hickman Browning*, ed. James G. Randall, 2 vols. (Springfield, Ill., 1925), 2: 559–60: entry of July 15, 1862.

18. *New York Herald*, July 7, 15, 1862. See also *New York World*, July 7, 8, 9, 1862, and *New York Times*, July 7, 10, 1862.

19. McClellan to Ellen Marcy McClellan, July 13, 22, 1862, George B. McClellan Papers, Library of Congress. Also printed in Sears, ed., *Civil War Papers of McClellan*, pp. 354, 368.

20. Oliver W. Norton to family, July 9, 13, 1862, in Norton, *Army Letters 1861–1865* (Chicago, 1903), pp. 98, 101.

21. John Gibbon to his wife, July 5, 1862, Gibbon Papers, Pennsylvania Historical Society; Thomas A. Tanfield to his sister, July 7, 1862, Tanfield Family Collection, U.S. Army Military History Institute, Carlisle, Pa. From the research notes of John Hennessy, used with permission.

22. Edward Acton to Mollie Acton, July 11, 1862, in " 'Dear Mollie': Letters

of Captain Edward A. Acton to His Wife, 1862," *Pennsylvania Magazine of History and Biography* 89 (1965): 35–36; Letter of Edward G. Abbott, July 12, in "Letters from the Harvard Regiments," ed. Anthony J. Milano, *Civil War: The Magazine of the Civil War Society* 13, p. 44, from the research notes of John Hennessy, used with permission.

23. All quotations from Bruce Tap, *Over Lincoln's Shoulder: The Committee on the Conduct of the War* (Lawrence, Kansas, 1998), pp. 122–25.

24. Brewster to his mother, July 9, 1862, Brewster to Mary Lou (sister), June 21, 1862, in *When This Cruel War Is Over: The Civil War Letters of Charles Harvey Brewster*, ed. David W. Blight (Amherst, Mass., 1992), pp. 163–64, 152; Kearny quoted in Bruce Catton, *Mr. Lincoln's Army* (Garden City, N.Y., 1951), p. 149.

25. Letter of Barlow dated July 12, 1862, Barlow Letters, Massachusetts Historical Society, from the research notes of John Hennessy, used with permission; Alfred Castleman diary, entries of July 13, Aug. 3, 1862, quoted in Kerry A. Trask, *Fire Within: A Civil War Narra-*

tive from Wisconsin (Kent, Ohio, 1995), p. 124.

26. Keyes to "My Dear Senator," July 5, 1862, Schoff Collection, Clements Library, University of Michigan, from the research notes of John Hennessy, used with permission.

27. *O.R.*, ser. 1, vol. 12, pt. 3, pp. 473–74.

28. Pope quoted by Salmon P. Chase, in *Inside Lincoln's Cabinet: The Civil War Diaries of Salmon P. Chase*, ed. David Donald (New York, 1954), p. 97: entry of July 21, 1862; Fitz-John Porter to J. C. G. Kennedy, July 17, Porter Papers, Library of Congress, from the research notes of John Hennessy, used with permission; George B. McClellan to Ellen Marcy McClellan, July 22, 1862, McClellan Papers, Library of Congress, also printed in Sears, ed., *Civil War Papers of McClellan*, p. 368.

29. McClellan to Samuel L. M. Barlow, July 23, 1862, Barlow Papers, the Huntington Library.

30. Roy P. Basler et al., eds., *The Collected Works of Abraham Lincoln*, 9 vols. (New Brunswick, N.J., 1953–1955), 5: 293–97.

31. *Constitutionnel*, June 7, 1862; *The Times*, June 23, 1862.

32. William L. Dayton to William H. Seward, June 12, 1862, *Papers Relating to Foreign Affairs, 1861–1862* (U.S. Department of State, Washington, 1862), pt. 1, pp. 349–50.

33. *Richmond Dispatch*, June 16, 1862; *New York Times*, July 10, 11, 12, 1862.

34. *The Diary of Edmund Ruffin*, ed. William Kauffman Scarborough, 3 vols. (Baton Rouge, 1972–1989), 2: 360, entry of June 30, 1862; *Richmond Dispatch*, July 4, 1862.

35. *New York Herald*, July 9, 1862; *New York Evening Post*, quoted in *Richmond Dispatch*, July 15, 1862. See also *New York Tribune*, July 2, 5, 1862; *New York Times*, July 11, 29, 1862; *New York World*, July 9, 1862.

36. *Constitutionnel*, July 19, 1862; Lynn M. Case and Warren F. Spencer, *The United States and France: Civil War Diplomacy* (Philadelphia, 1970), pp. 300–307.

37. *The Times*, July 17, Aug. 15, 1862; *Morning Post*, quoted in *New York Tribune*, July 30, 1862.

38. Bright to Sumner, July 12, 1862; Cobden to Sumner, July 11, 1862, quoted in James Ford Rhodes, *History of the United States from the Compromise*

of 1850 to the McKinley–Bryan Campaign of 1896, 8 vols. (New York, 1920), 4: 85n.

39. De Gasparin to Lincoln, July 18, 1862, Lincoln to de Gasparin, Aug. 4, 1862, in *Collected Works of Lincoln*, 5: 355–56.

40. Henry Adams to Charles Francis Adams Jr., July 19, 1862, in *A Cycle of Adams Letters, 1861–1865*, ed. Worthing- ton Chauncey Ford, 2 vols. (Boston, 1920), 1: 166.

41. Ephraim Douglass Adams, *Great Britain and the American Civil War*, 2 vols. (New York, 1925), 2: 20–23; Howard Jones, *Union in Peril: The Crisis over British Intervention in the Civil War* (Chapel Hill, N.C., 1992), p. 136.

42. James Mason to his wife, July 20, 1862, in Virginia Mason, *The Public Life and Diplomatic Correspondence of James M. Mason* (New York, 1906), p. 281; John Slidell to Judah P. Benjamin, July 25, 1862, quoted in Case and Spencer, *The United States and France*, p. 310.

43. William L. Yancey and A. Dudley Mann to Robert Toombs, May 21, 1861, in *A Compilation of the Messages*

and *Papers of the Confederacy*, comp. James D. Richardson, 2 vols. (Nashville, 1906), 2: 37; Lincoln quoted in *The Reminiscences of Carl Schurz*, 3 vols. (New York, 1907–1908), 2: 309.

44. *Saturday Review*, Sept. 14, 1861, quoted in Adams, *Great Britain and the American Civil War*, 2: 181; *Economist*, Sept. 1861, quoted in Karl Marx and Friedrich Engels, *The Civil War in the United States*, ed. Richard Enmale (New York, 1937), p. 12; *Reynolds Weekly Newspaper*, Summer 1861, quoted in G. D. Lillibridge, *Beacon of Freedom: The Impact of American Democracy upon Great Britain 1830–1870* (Philadelphia, 1955), p. 115.

45. *The Journal of Benjamin Moran, 1857–1865* (Chicago, 1949), p. 1042: entry of July 19, 1862.

46. Lincoln to Albert G. Hodges, April 4, 1864, *Collected Works of Lincoln*, 7: 281.

47. *Douglass' Monthly* 4 (July 1861), 486; *Montgomery Advertiser*, Nov. 6, 1861.

48. Charles Brewster to his mother, March 4, 1862, in Blight, ed., *When This Cruel War Is Over*, p. 92; John C. Buchanan to Sophia Buchanan, Oct. 17, 1861, in "The Negro as Viewed by

a Michigan Civil War Soldier: Letters of John C. Buchanan," ed. George M. Blackburn, *Michigan History* 47 (1963): 79–80.

49. Charles Wills to family, April 16, 1862, Wills to his brother, Feb. 25, 1862, in *Army Life of an Illinois Soldier: Letters and Diary of the Late Charles Wills* (Washington, 1906), pp. 83, 158; Henry Andrews to Susan Andrews, Sept. 9, 1862, Andrews Papers, Illinois State Historical Library.

50. Douglass to Charles Sumner, April 8, 1862, Sumner Papers, Houghton Library, Harvard University; Unknown to Christopher A. Fleetwood, April 12, 1862, Fleetwood Papers, Library of Congress.

51. *Collected Works of Lincoln*, 5: 144–46.

52. Charles M. Segal, ed., *Conversations with Lincoln* (New York, 1961), pp. 164–68; Basler et al., eds., *Collected Works of Lincoln*, 5: 223.

53. John Beatty, *Memoirs of a Volunteer 1861–1863*, ed. Harvey S. Ford (New York, 1946), p. 118: diary entry of July 18, 1862; John Sherman to William Tecumseh Sherman, Aug. 24, 1862, in *Life in the North During the Civil War*, ed. George Winston Smith and

Charles Judah (Albuquerque, 1966), p. 99.

54. Illinois officer quoted in Bruce Catton, *Grant Moves South* (Boston, 1960), p. 294; Brewster to Mary Brewster, May 18, June 21, in Blight, ed., *When This Cruel War Is Over*, pp. 133, 152; the Iowa private was George Lowe, writing to his wife Elizabeth Lowe, Aug. 17, 1862, Lowe Papers, the Huntington Library. For an astute study of the emergence of "hard war" attitudes in the Union army, see Mark Grimsley, *The Hard Hand of War: Union Military Policy toward Southern Civilians, 1861–1865* (New York, 1995).

55. Halleck to Grant, Aug. 2, 1862, in *O.R.*, ser. 1, vol. 17, pt. 2, p. 150.

56. Stephen O. Himoe to his wife, June 26, 1862, in "An Army Surgeon's Letters to His Wife," ed. Luther M. Kuhns, *Proceedings of the Mississippi Valley Historical Association* 7 (1914): 311–12; Lucius Hubbard to Mary Hubbard, Sept. 8, 1862, in "Letters of a Union Officer: L. F. Hubbard and the Civil War," ed. N. B. Martin, *Minnesota History* 35 (1957): 314–15.

57. *O.R.*, ser. 1, vol. 12, pt. 2, pp. 50–52.

58. *New York Times*, July 27, 1862.
59. Freeman, R. E. Lee, 2: 264; McClellan to Ellen Marcy McClellan, July 17, 1862, McClellan Papers, Library of Congress, printed also in Sears, ed., *Civil War Papers of McClellan*, p. 362.
60. *O.R.*, ser. 1, vol. 11, pt. 1, pp. 73–74.
61. Porter to Manton Marble, May 21, 1862, Marble Papers, Library of Congress, from the research notes of John Hennessy, used with permission; Keyes to Montgomery Meigs, Aug. 21, 1862, Meigs Papers, Library of Congress, from the research notes of John Hennessy, used with permission.
62. Basler et al., eds., *Collected Works of Lincoln*, 5: 49.
63. Lincoln to Cuthbert Bullitt, July 28, 1862, Lincoln to August Belmont, July 31, 1862, in Basler et al., eds., *Collected Works of Lincoln*, 5: 344–46, 350–51.
64. John Sherman to William T. Sherman, Aug. 24, 1862, in *The Sherman Letters: Correspondence between General and Senator Sherman from 1837 to 1891*, ed. Rachel S. Thorndike (New York, 1894), pp. 156–57; *Boston Advertiser*, Aug. 20, 1862.

65. Basler et al., eds., *Collected Works of Lincoln*, 5: 317–19.
66. Gideon Welles, "The History of Emancipation," *The Galaxy* 14 (1872), 842–43.
67. Basler et al., eds., *Collected Works of Lincoln*, 5: 336–37; Francis B. Carpenter, *Six Months at the White House with Abraham Lincoln* (New York, 1866), pp. 20–22.
68. Carpenter, *Six Months at the White House*, p. 22.

THREE

1. Isaac N. Brown, "The Confederate Gun-Boat 'Arkansas,' " in *Battles and Leaders of the Civil War*, ed. Clarence C. Buel and Robert U. Johnson, 4 vols. (New York, 1888), 3: 576.
2. *Richmond Enquirer*, July 21, 1862; *Richmond Dispatch*, July 31, 1862; *The Journals of Josiah Gorgas, 1857–1878*, ed. Sarah Woolfolk Wiggins (Tuscaloosa, Ala., 1995), p. 49: entry of July 27, 1862.
3. *Richmond Enquirer*, July 31, 1862; Bragg to P. G. T. Beauregard, July 22, 1862, quoted in Shelby Foote, *The Civil War: A Narrative. Fort Sumter to Perryville* (New York, 1958), p. 571.

4. Frank Moore, *The Rebellion Record*, vol. 5 (New York, 1863), sec. 1: "Diary of Events," p. 72.
5. *New York World*, Sept. 9, 1862; Charles Francis Adams Jr. to Charles Francis Adams, Aug. 27, 1862, in *A Cycle of Adams Letters 1861–1865*, ed. Worthington Chauncey Ford, 2 vols. (Boston, 1920), 1: 177–78.
6. *The Diary of Orville Hickman Browning*, ed. James G. Randall, 2 vols. (Springfield, Ill., 1925), 1: 563.
7. The best account of this exchange is Stephen W. Sears, *George B. McClellan: The Young Napoleon* (New York, 1988), pp. 238–42. For the correspondence on this and related matters, see Stephen W. Sears, ed., *The Civil War Papers of George B. McClellan: Selected Correspondence, 1860–1865* (New York, 1989), pp. 369–93.
8. McClellan to Ellen Marcy McClellan, Aug. 10, 1862, McClellan Papers, Library of Congress; also in Sears, ed., *Civil War Papers of McClellan*, pp. 389–90.
9. Charles H. Brewster to Mary Brewster, July 27, 1862, in *When This Cruel War Is Over: The Civil War Letters of Charles Harvey Brewster*, ed. David

W. Blight (Amherst, Mass., 1992), p. 177; New York officer quoted in Nancy S. Garrison, *With Courage and Delicacy: Civil War on the Peninsula* (Mason City, Iowa, 1999), p. 12.

10. McClellan to Ellen Marcy McClellan, Aug. 10, 23, 24, 1862, McClellan Papers; also in Sears, *Civil War Papers of McClellan*, pp. 389, 400, 404.

11. Porter to J. Howard Foote, Aug. 12, Porter Papers, Library of Congress, quoted in Bruce Tap, *Over Lincoln's Shoulder: The Committee on the Conduct of the War* (Lawrence, Kans., 1998), p. 131; Porter to Manton Marble, Aug. 10, 1862, Marble Papers, Library of Congress, quoted in T. Harry Williams, *Lincoln and His Generals* (New York, 1952), p. 148.

12. Taylor to Mary Lou Taylor, Aug. 31, 1862, in *Lee's Adjutant: The Wartime Letters of Colonel Walter Herron Taylor, 1862–1865*, ed. R. Lockwood Tower (Columbia, S.C., 1995), p. 41.

13. This remarkable series of telegrams and events is conveniently reprinted and chronicled in Sears, ed., *Civil War Papers of McClellan*, pp. 410–19.

14. Charles Wolcott quoted in John J. Hennessy, *Return to Bull Run: The*

Campaign and Battle of Second Manassas (New York, 1993), p. 437; *The Reminiscences of Carl Schurz*, 3 vols. (New York, 1907–1908), 2: 382.

15. McClellan to Lincoln, Aug. 29, 1862, in Sears, ed., *Civil War Papers of McClellan*, p. 416; *Inside Lincoln's White House: The Complete Civil War Diary of John Hay*, ed. Michael Burlingame and John R. Turner Ettlinger (Carbondale, Ill., 1997), pp. 36–37: entry of Sept. 1, 1862; John G. Nicolay and John Hay, *Abraham Lincoln: A History*, 10 vols. (New York, 1890), 6: 16.

16. Quoted in Stephen W. Sears, *Landscape Turned Red: The Battle of Antietam* (New Haven, 1983), p. 13.

17. Quotations from *New York Tribune*, Sept. 4, 1862; *New York Times*, Sept. 5, 1862. See also the following (all dates in 1862): *New York Herald*, Sept. 5; *New York World*, Sept. 1, 5; *New York Sunday Mercury*, Sept. 7; *Elizabeth (N.J.) Unionist*, Sept. 13; *Chicago Times*, Sept. 11.

18. *New York Herald*, Sept. 5, 1862; *Baltimore American*, quoted in *Richmond Enquirer*, Sept. 9, 1862.

19. *The Diary of George Templeton Strong*,

Vol. 3: The Civil War 1860–1865, ed. Allan Nevins and Milton Halsey Thomas (New York, 1952), pp. 251–53: entries of Sept. 3 and 7, 1862; *New York Times*, Sept. 7, 1862.

20. Henry Pearson to "friend," Sept. 5, 1862, in *The Brothers' War: Civil War Letters to Their Loved Ones from the Blue and Gray*, ed. Annette Tapert (New York, 1988), p. 85; Washington Roebling to his father, early September, in *Tragic Years 1860–1865*, ed. Paul M. Angle and Earl Schenck Miers, 2 vols. (New York, 1960), 1: 344–45; Francis Barlow to his mother, Sept. 6, 1862, in James V. Murfin, *The Gleam of Bayonets: The Battle of Antietam and Robert E. Lee's Maryland Campaign, September 1862* (Baton Rouge, 1965), p. 83.

21. Orlando Poe to his wife, Sept. 4, 1862, in Hennessy, *Return to Bull Run*, p. 454; *Inside Lincoln's Army: The Diary of General Marsena Rudolph Patrick*, ed. Davis S. Sparks (New York, 1964), p. 140: entry of Sept. 6, 1862.

22. Adams Hill to Sidney Howard Gay, Aug. 31, 1862, quoted in Burlingame and Ettlinger, eds., *Inside Lincoln's White House*, p. 293n.; and John Hay's

diary entry of Sept. 1, 1862, from ibid., pp. 36–37.

23. *Diary of Gideon Welles,* ed. Howard K. Beale, 3 vols. (New York, 1960), 1: 93–102: entries of Aug. 31 and Sept. 1, 1862; *The Salmon P. Chase Papers, Vol. 1: Journals, 1829–1872,* ed. John Niven (Kent, Ohio, 1993), pp. 366–68: diary entries of Aug. 29, 30, 31, Sept. 1, 1862.
24. McClellan to Ellen Marcy McClellan, Sept. 5, 8, 1862, McClellan Papers; also in Sears, ed., *Civil War Papers of McClellan,* pp. 435, 440.
25. *Diary of Gideon Welles,* 1: 104–5: entries of Sept. 2 and 7, 1862; *Inside Lincoln's White House,* pp. 38–39, entry of Sept. 5, 1862; *The Collected Works of Abraham Lincoln,* ed. Roy P. Basler and others, 9 vols. (New Brunswick, N.J., 1953–1955), 5: 48n.: notation on Sept. 2 Cabinet meeting by Attorney-General Edward Bates.
26. William H. Powell and George Kimball quoted in Buel and Johnson, eds., *Battles and Leaders of the Civil War,* 2: 490n. and 550–51n.; *War Diary and Letters of Stephen Minot Weld 1861–1865* (Boston, 1912), letter of Weld to his father, Sept. 4, 1862, p. 136.

27. *Chicago Tribune*, Sept. 9, 1862.
28. Lee to Jefferson Davis, Sept. 3, 1862, in *The Wartime Papers of R. E. Lee*, ed. Clifford Dowdey and Louis H. Manarin (New York, 1961), p. 27.
29. For analyses of Lee's motives and goals in this campaign, see Douglas Southall Freeman, *R. E. Lee: A Biography*, 4 vols. (New York, 1934–1935), 2: 350–53; Joseph L. Harsh, *Confederate Tide Rising: Robert E. Lee and the Making of Southern Strategy, 1861–1862* (Kent, Ohio, 1998), pp. 1–4; Joseph L. Harsh, *Taken at the Flood: Robert E. Lee and Confederate Strategy in the Maryland Campaign of 1862* (Kent, Ohio, 1999), chaps. 1–3; Michael A. Palmer, *Lee Moves North: Robert E. Lee on the Offensive* (New York, 1998), chap. 1; and D. Scott Hartwig, "Robert E. Lee and the Maryland Campaign," in *Lee the Soldier*, ed. Gary W. Gallagher (Lincoln, Neb., 1996), pp. 331–36.
30. *Richmond Dispatch*, Aug. 29, Sept. 11, 1862; diary of James W. Shinn, copy in 4th North Carolina file, Antietam National Battlefield Library, entry of Aug. 30, 1862.
31. *Richmond Enquirer*, Sept. 5, 9, 1862;

Richmond Examiner, Sept. 5, 1862.

32. *Shadows on My Heart: The Civil War Diary of Lucy Rebecca Buck of Virginia,* ed. Elizabeth R. Baer (Athens, Ga., 1997), pp. 144–45: entry of Aug. 31, 1862; Charles C. Jones Jr. to Charles C. Jones, Sept. 10, 1862, in *Children of Pride: A True Story of Georgia and the Civil War,* ed. Robert Manson Myers (New Haven, 1972), pp. 962–63; *Richmond Examiner,* Sept. 5, 1862.

33. Charles C. Jones Jr. to his mother, Sept. 8, 1862, *Children of Pride,* p. 960.

34. *O.R.,* series I, vol. 19, pt. 2, pp. 596, 601–2.

35. Lee to Davis, Sept. 8, 1862, in Dowdey and Manarin, eds., *Wartime Papers of Lee,* p. 301.

36. *Newark Journal* quoted in *Richmond Dispatch,* Aug. 2, 1862; *Cincinnati Gazette,* Oct. 17, 1862, quoted in Allan Nevins, *The War for the Union, vol. 2: War Becomes Revolution* (New York, 1960), p. 322; Seymour quoted in *Richmond Dispatch,* July 24, 1862.

37. *Richmond Dispatch,* July 24, 1862.

38. *New York Times,* Sept. 22, 1862.

39. Howard Jones, *Abraham Lincoln and the New Birth of Freedom* (Lincoln, Neb., 1999), p. 96. See also Maria

Lydig Daly, *Diary of a Union Lady 1861–1865*, ed. Harold Earl Hammond (New York, 1962), p. 182: entry of Oct. 4, 1862; and Howard Jones, *Union in Peril: The Crisis over British Intervention in the Civil War* (Chapel Hill, N.C., 1992), p. 206.

40. Frank L. Owsley, *King Cotton Diplomacy: Foreign Relations of the Confederate States of America* (Chicago, 1931), p. 353.

41. *The Journal of Benjamin Moran, 1857–1865*, 2 vols. (Chicago, 1949), 2: 1071–73: entries of Sept. 13, 15, 17, 20, 1862.

42. William L. Dayton to William H. Seward, Sept. 17, 1862, quoted in Jones, *Lincoln and the New Birth of Freedom*, p. 98; Gladstone to Lord John Russell, Aug. 30, 1862, Gladstone to William Stuart, Sept. 8, 1862, Gladstone Letterbook, quoted in ibid., p. 93.

43. This exchange is conveniently reprinted in Murfin, *The Gleam of Bayonets*, pp. 394, 396–97, from the Russell Papers, Public Record Office, London.

44. Palmerston to Gladstone, Sept. 24, 1862, in *Gladstone and Palmerston,*

Being the Correspondence of Lord Palmerston with Mr. Gladstone, 1861–1865, ed. Phillip Guedalla (Covent Garden, 1928), pp. 232–33.

45. Russell to Henry R. C. Wellesley, Earl of Cowley (the British Ambassador to France), Sept. 26, 1862, in Frank Merli and Theodore A. Wilson, "The British Cabinet and the Confederacy: Autumn, 1862," *Maryland Historical Magazine* 65 (1970): 247n.; Palmerston to Russell, Sept. 23, 1862, Russell Papers, reprinted in Murfin, *Gleam of Bayonets*, p. 400; Palmerston to Gladstone, Sept. 24, 1862, in Guedalla, ed., *Gladstone and Palmerston*, p. 233.

46. Taylor to Mary Lou Taylor, Sept. 7, 1862, in Tower, ed., *Lee's Adjutant*, p. 43.

FOUR

1. Taylor to Mary Lou Taylor, Sept. 7, 1862, in *Lee's Adjutant: The Wartime Letters of Colonel Walter Herron Taylor*, ed. R. Lockwood Tower (Columbia, S.C., 1995), p. 43; Milton Barrett to his brother and sister, Sept. 9, 1862, in *The Confederacy Is on Her Way Up the Spout: Letters to South Carolina, 1861–1864*, ed. J. Roderick Heller III and

Carolynn Ayres Heller (Athens, Ga., 1992), p. 74.

2. *Richmond Dispatch*, Sept. 11, 1862; *Richmond Whig*, Sept. 13, 1862; *Richmond Enquirer*, Sept. 16, 1862.
3. *Richmond Examiner*, Sept. 23, 1862; letter of James S. Johnston, quoted in John M. Priest, *Antietam: The Soldiers' Battle* (Shippensburg, Pa., 1989), p. 4.
4. Richard Wheeler, ed., *Lee's Terrible Swift Sword: From Antietam to Chancellorsville, An Eyewitness History* (New York, 1992), pp. 54–55.
5. Mary Bedinger Mitchell, "A Woman's Recollections of Antietam," in *Battles and Leaders of the Civil War*, ed. Clarence G. Buel and Robert U. Johnson, 4 vols. (New York, 1888), 2: 687–88.
6. Union surgeon quoted in *The Civil War: The American Iliad as Told by Those Who Lived It*, ed. Otto Eisenschiml and Ralph Newman, 2 vols. (New York, 1956), 1: 262; Frederick civilian quoted in Wheeler, *Lee's Terrible Swift Sword*, p. 55.
7. Quoted in Joseph L. Harsh, *Taken at the Flood: Robert E. Lee and Confederate Strategy in the Maryland Campaign of 1862* (Kent, Ohio, 1999), p. 74.
8. *The Journals of Josiah Gorgas, 1857–*

1878, ed. Sarah Woolfolk Wiggins (Tuscaloosa, Ala., 1995), entry of September 14, 1862.

9. Kate Stone, *Brokenburn: The Journal of Kate Stone, 1861–1868*, ed. John Q. Anderson (Baton Rouge, 1955), p. 142: entry of Sept. 23, 1862; *"Journal of a Secesh Lady": The Diary of Catherine Ann Devereux Edmondston, 1860–1866*, ed. Beth Gilbert Crabtree and James W. Patton (Raleigh, N.C., 1979), p. 251: entry of Sept. 9, 1862.

10. *Richmond Dispatch*, Sept. 17, 1862.

11. Frank Moore, *The Rebellion Record*, vol. 5 (New York, 1863), sec. 1: "Diary of Events," pp. 73–78, a compilation of reports from Pennsylvania newspapers and other sources; Sidney Howard Gay to Adams S. Hill, c. Sept. 10, 1862, in James Ford Rhodes, *History of the United States from the Compromise of 1850 to the McKinley–Bryan Campaign of 1896*, 8 vols. (New York, 1920), 4: 144n.; Charles Loring Brace to Frederick Law Olmsted, Sept. 12, 1862, in *The Papers of Frederick Law Olmsted*, vol. 4: *Defending the Union*, ed. Jane Turner Censor (Baltimore, 1986), p. 415.

12. *New York World*, Sept. 10, 1862; *New*

York Times, Sept. 13, 1862; *New York Herald*, Sept. 13, 1862.

13. Meade to his wife, Sept. 12, 1862, in George G. Meade, *Life and Letters of George Gordon Meade*, 2 vols. (New York, 1913), 1: 309; Charles Merrick to Myra Merrick, Sept. 9, Merrick Papers, Western Reserve Historical Society, Cleveland.

14. *Hard Marching Every Day: The Civil War Letters of Private Wilbur Fisk, 1861–1865*, ed. Emil and Ruth Rosenblatt (Lawrence, Kans., 1992), letter dated Sept. 9, 1862.

15. Williams to his daughter, Sept. 8, 12, 1862, in *From the Cannon's Mouth: The Civil War Letters of Alpheus S. Williams* (Detroit, 1959), pp. 111, 120–21.

16. Elizabeth Blair Lee to Samuel Phillips Lee, Sept. 8, 15, 1862, in *Wartime Washington: The Civil War Letters of Elizabeth Blair Lee*, ed. Virginia Jeans Laas (Urbana, Ill., 1991), pp. 177, 182.

17. Quoted in Bruce Catton, *Mr. Lincoln's Army* (Garden City, N.Y., 1951), p. 167.

18. James Anderson, diary entry of Sept. 14, 1862; Dr. Alfred Castleman, diary entry of Sept. 12, 1862, both in Kerry

A. Trask, *Fire Within: A Civil War Narrative from Wisconsin* (Kent, Ohio, 1995), p. 127.

19. James Bell to Augusta Hallock, Sept. 22, 1862, in James Alvin Bell Papers, The Huntington Library.

20. Ibid.; *A Virginia Yankee in the Civil War: The Diaries of David Hunter Strother*, ed. Cecil D. Eby (Chapel Hill, N.C., 1961), p. 150: entry of Sept. 13, 1862.

21. Gibbon to his wife, Sept. 16, 1862, Gibbon Papers, Pennsylvania Historical Society, from the research notes of John Hennessy, used with permission; Thomas Francis Galwey, *The Valiant Hours*, ed. W. S. Nye (Harrisburg, Pa., 1961), p. 35. Several soldiers used the same "God's country" expression. Writing a description of his war experiences for his children more than forty years later, a veteran of the 104th New York recalled that the regiment's reception in Maryland "seemed like getting into God's country again." H. W. Burlingame, typescript memoirs, 1904, pp. 34–35, copy in 104th New York file, Antietam National Battlefield Library.

22. Letter of James Rush Holmes, Sept. 9,

1862, in "Civil War Letters of James Rush Holmes," ed. Ida Bright Adams, *Western Pennsylvania Historical Magazine* 44 (1965): 117; Mark De Wolfe Howe, ed., *Touched With Fire: Civil War Letters and Diary of Oliver Wendell Holmes, Jr., 1861–1864* (Cambridge, Mass., 1946), p. 64.

23. Perry Mayo to his father, Sept. 7, 1862, in "The Civil War Letters of Perry Mayo," *Michigan State University Museum Cultural Series* 1 (1967), p. 217; Josiah M. Favill, *Diary of a Young Officer* (Chicago, 1909), pp. 182–83: entry of Sept. 6, 1862.

24. Stephen W. Sears, *Landscape Turned Red: The Battle of Antietam* (New Haven, 1983), p. 90.

25. For analyses of events described in this and the following paragraphs, see James V. Murfin, *The Gleam of Bayonets: The Battle of Antietam and the Maryland Campaign of 1862* (Baton Rouge, 1965), pp. 328–38; Sears, *Landscape Turned Red*, pp. 349–52; and Stephen W. Sears, "Last Words on the Lost Order," in the same author's *Controversies and Commanders: Dispatches from the Army of the Potomac* (Boston, 1999), pp. 109–30.

26. John Gibbon, *Personal Recollections of the Civil War* (New York, 1928), p. 73. Colonel Silas Colgrove of the 27th Indiana claimed that Pittman had served with Chilton in the pre-war army and recognized his handwriting (Colgrove, "The Finding of Lee's Lost Order," in Buel and Johnson, *Battles and Leaders of the Civil War*, 2: 603). But Sears, "Last Words on the Lost Order," p. 115, shows that while Pittman knew of Chilton before the war, he had not served with him. Sears, however, does not specify how Pittman or anyone else validated the genuineness of the orders.

27. Walter H. Taylor, *Four Years With General Lee*, ed. James I. Robertson Jr. (Bloomington, Ind., 1962), p. 67; *O.R.*, ser. 1, vol. 19, pt. 2, p. 281.

28. Henry Kyd Douglas, "Stonewall Jackson in Maryland," Buel and Johnson, *Battles and Leaders of the Civil War*, 2: 627. Paul R. Teetor, *A Matter of Hours: Treason at Harper's Ferry* (Rutherford, N.J., 1982), argues from circumstantial evidence that Miles deliberately sabotaged the defense of the garrison. A retired judge who presented his argument in the manner of

a brief against Miles, Teetor cannot be said to have "proved" his case though he raised several disturbing questions.

29. Thomas L. Livermore, *Numbers and Losses in the Civil War in America 1861–65* (Boston, 1900), counts a minimum of 2,685 Confederate casualties. Ezra Carman, who made an exhaustive study of the Antietam campaign in the 1880s and 1890s, counted only 1,932 Confederate casualties at Turner's and Fox's Gaps. Carman, "The Maryland Campaign of 1862," unpublished typescript, copy in the Antietam National Battlefield Library, chap. 26, p. 2. Both Livermore and Carman fought at Antietam, Liver- more as a lieutenant in the 5th New Hampshire and Carman as colonel of the 13th New Jersey.
30. *O.R.*, ser. 1, vol. 51, pt. 2, pp. 618–19.
31. Ibid., vol. 19, pt. 2, pp. 289, 294–95.
32. *New York World*, Sept. 16, 1862; *Baltimore American*, Sept. 15, 1862; *New York Herald*, Sept. 16, 1862.
33. Roy P. Basler et al., eds., *The Collected Works of Abraham Lincoln*, 9 vols. (New Brunswick, N.J., 1953–1955), 5: 246.
34. Harsh, *Taken at the Flood*, p. 288.
35. Ibid., p. 305.

36. Keith S. Bohannon, "Dirty, Ragged, and Ill-Provided For: Confederate Logistical Problems in the 1862 Maryland Campaign and Their Solutions," in *The Antietam Campaign*, ed. Gary W. Gallagher (Chapel Hill, N.C., 1999), p. 114.

37. McClellan to Ellen Marcy McClellan, Sept. 16, 1862, McClellan Papers, Library of Congress; also printed in *The Civil War Papers of George B. McClellan: Selected Correspondence, 1860–1865*, ed. Stephen W. Sears (New York, 1989), p. 466.

38. James B. Casey, ed., "The Ordeal of Adoniram Judson Warner: His Minutes of South Mountain and Antietam," *Civil War History* 28 (1982): 218–19.

39. Letter of George Breck dated Sept. 18, 1862, in *Rochester Union and Advertiser*, Sept. 26, from the research notes of John Hennessy, used with permission.

40. Hooker quoted in *New York Times*, Sept. 20, 1862; Williams to his daughters, Sept. 22, 1862, in *From the Cannon's Mouth*, p. 125.

41. Rufus R. Dawes, *Service with the Sixth Wisconsin Volunteers* (Madison, 1890),

pp. 90–91. The 6th Wisconsin lost forty killed or mortally wounded and 112 wounded at Antietam, nearly 50 percent of the men who went into the battle.

42. *O.R.*, ser. 1, vol. 19, pt. 1, p. 218.

43. James A. Lemon diary: entry of Sept. 18, 1862, 18th Georgia file, Antietam National Battlefield Library.

44. Stephen Elliott Welch to parents, Sept. 22, Hampton Legion file, Antietam National Battlefield Library; undated account by Lt. Col. P. A. Work in 1st Texas file, Antietam National Battlefield Library; Hood quoted in G. F. R. Henderson, *Stonewall Jackson and the American Civil War* (repr. ed., New York, 1988), p. 541.

45. Andrew E. Ford, diary entry of Oct. 8, 1862, 15th Massachusetts File, Antietam National Battlefield Library.

46. Jonathan P. Stowe diary: entry of Sept. 17, 1862, 15th Massachusetts file, Antietam National Battlefield Library.

47. Thomas L. Livermore, *Days and Events, 1860–1866* (Boston, 1920), p. 141.

48. Frederick Tilbert, *Antietam* (Washington, 1961), p. 39; Edward Porter

Alexander, *Military Memoirs of a Confederate*, ed. T. Harry Williams (Bloomington, Ind., 1962), p. 262.

49. Catton, *Mr. Lincoln's Army*, p. 304.

50. *O.R.*, ser. 1, vol. 19, pt. 1, p. 377.

51. The Graham quotations are from the research notes of John Hennessy, used with permission, and from a letter of Graham to Rush C. Hawkins, Sept. 27, 1894, Brown University Library, copy in the 9th New York file, Antietam National Battlefield Library.

52. David L. Thompson, "With Burnside at Antietam," in Buel and Johnson, eds., *Battles and Leaders of the Civil War*, 2: 661–62.

53. Murfin, *Gleam of Bayonets*, p. 282.

54. D. Scott Hartwig, "Who Would Not Be a Soldier: The Volunteers of '62 in the Maryland Campaign," in Gallagher, ed., *The Antietam Campaign*, p. 143.

55. For Porter's quoted remark and the surrounding controversy, see Buel and Johnson, eds., *Battles and Leaders of the Civil War*, 2: 656n. The civilian was a Baltimore merchant, quoted in the *Baltimore American*, Sept. 20, 1862.

56. For the higher estimate of Confederate casualties, see Livermore, *Num-*

bers and Losses, pp. 92–93; for the lower estimate, see Carman, "The Maryland Campaign of 1862," chap. 26. Sears, *Landscape Turned Red,* p. 296, accepts Carman's estimate, but adds that many of the 753 Union soldiers and 1,018 Confederate soldiers listed as "missing" were undoubtedly killed. The casualty figures for Confederates tabulated in Buel and Johnson, *Battles and Leaders of the Civil War,* 2: 603, are 1,512 killed, 7,816 wounded, and 1,844 missing. Confederates tended to underreport their casualties, and the Carman and *Battles and Leaders* totals are perhaps too low, while Livermore's figures are almost certainly too high. A fair estimate of the number of Confederates killed outright (including some of the missing) would be 2,000; the total for the Union (including some of the missing) would be about 2,300. At least 2,000 of the combined total of 17,300 wounded died of their wounds, making an estimated total of 6,300 to 6,500 killed and mortally wounded in the single bloodiest day of American history.

57. Quoted in Sears, *Landscape Turned Red,* p. 315.

58. *O.R.*, ser. 1, vol. 19, pt. 2, p. 322. The number of Confederates in line on September 18 included stragglers who had been brought up overnight, mostly from A. P. Hill's division.

59. *O.R.*, ser. 1, vol. 19, pt. 1, pp. 32, 65.

60. Diary of James A. Lemon: entry of Sept. 18, 1862, in 18th Georgia File, Antietam National Battlefield Library.

61. *O.R.*, ser. 1, vol. 19, pt. 2, p. 330.

62. George H. Nye to his wife, Sept. 21, 1862, letter in possession of Nicholas C. Picerno of Claremont, N.H., used with permission; John H. Burnham to his mother, Oct. 4, 1862, 16th Connecticut file, Antietam National Battlefield Library; Thomas Welsh to his wife, Sept. 21, 1862, 45th Pennsylvania file, Antietam National Battlefield Library.

63. *Diary of Gideon Welles*, ed. Howard K. Beale, 3 vols. (New York, 1960), 1: 140.

64. McClellan to Ellen Marcy McClellan, Sept. 20, 1862, McClellan Papers, Library of Congress; also in Sears, ed., *Civil War Papers of McClellan*, p. 473.

FIVE

1. Joseph L. Harsh, *Taken at the Flood:*

Robert E. Lee and Confederate Strategy in the Maryland Campaign of 1862 (Kent, Ohio, 1999), pp. 432–33.

2. Taylor to Mary Lou Taylor, Sept. 28, 1862, in *Lee's Adjutant: The Wartime Letters of Colonel Walter Herron Taylor,* ed. R. Lockwood Tower (Columbia, S.C., 1995), p. 45; *O.R.,* ser. 1, vol. 19, pt. 2, pp. 626–27.

3. Shepherd Pryor to his wife, Sept. 23, 1862, in *The Antietam Campaign,* ed. Gary W. Gallagher (Chapel Hill, N.C., 1999), p. 22; letter of William Stillwell, undated, from the research notes of John Hennessy, used with permission.

4. Taylor to Mary Lou Taylor, Sept. 21, 1862, in Tower, ed., *Lee's Adjutant,* pp. 44–45.

5. Gibbon to his wife, Sept. 21, 1862, Gibbon Papers, Pennsylvania Historical Society, from the research notes of John Hennessy, used with permission; George Breck's letter dated Sept. 18, 1862, published in the *Rochester Union and Advertiser,* Sept. 26, from the research notes of John Hennessy, used with permission; Williams to "My Dear Lew," Sept. 24, 1862, in *From the Cannon's Mouth: The Civil War Letters of Alpheus S. Williams,* ed. Milo M.

Quaife (Detroit, 1959), pp. 134–35.

6. Willcox to Marie Willcox, Oct. 2, 1862, in *Forgotten Valor: The Memoirs, Journals, and Civil War Letters of Orlando B. Willcox*, ed. Robert Garth Scott (Kent, Ohio, 1999), p. 369; Frank Lindley Lemont to "Dear Cousin Augusta," Oct. 17, 1862, from the research notes of John Hennessy, used with permission.

7. *New York Sunday Mercury*, Sept. 21, 1862, reprinted in *Writing and Fighting the Civil War: Soldier Correspondence to the New York Sunday Mercury*, ed. William B. Styple (Kearny, N.J., 2000), pp. 124–25; *New York Times*, Sept. 18, 20, 21, 1862.

8. *New York World*, Sept. 19, 1862; *New York Times*, Sept. 20, 1862.

9. *New York Times*, Sept. 20, 21, 1862; *New York Herald*, Sept. 21, 1862; *New York World*, Sept. 20, 1862.

10. *Harper's Weekly*, Oct. 4, 1862.

11. *Shadows on My Heart: The Civil War Diary of Lucy Rebecca Buck of Virginia*, ed. Elizabeth R. Baer (Athens, Ga., 1997), p. 151: entry of Sept. 20, 1862; Charles C. Jones Jr. to Charles C. Jones, Sept. 27, 1862, in *Children of Pride: A True Story of Georgia and the*

Civil War, ed. Robert Manson Myers (New Haven, 1972), p. 966.

12. *Richmond Enquirer*, Sept. 23, 1862; *Richmond Dispatch*, Sept. 23, 24, 1862.

13. *Richmond Dispatch*, Sept. 23, 1862; *Richmond Enquirer*, Sept. 24, 1862.

14. *Richmond Dispatch*, Sept. 26, 20, 1862; *Richmond Enquirer*, Sept. 24, 1862.

15. Gary W. Gallagher, "The Net Result of the Campaign Was in Our Favor," in Gallagher, ed., *The Antietam Campaign*, pp. 3–43. See also *The Diary of Edmund Ruffin*, 3 vols., ed. William Kauffman Scarborough (Baton Rouge, 1972–1989), 2: 449–50: entry of Sept. 23, 1862: "The great balance of gain must be on our side."

16. *Richmond Dispatch*, Oct. 9, 1862. See also *Richmond Enquirer*, Oct. 7, 1862.

17. *Richmond Dispatch*, Oct. 15, 1862.

18. *Inside the Confederate Government: The Diary of Robert Garlick Hill Kean*, ed. Edward Younger (New York, 1957), p. 86: entry of June 27, 1863. Davis made this remark to Secretary of War George Wythe Randolph in October 1862; Randolph later quoted Davis to his nephew-in-law Kean, who was chief of the Bureau of War.

19. Maria Lydig Daly, *Diary of a Union*

Lady 1861–1865, ed. Harold Earl Hammond (New York, 1962), p. 174: entry of Sept. 19, 1862; *The Diary of George Templeton Strong, Vol. 3: The Civil War, 1860–1865*, ed. Allan Nevins and Milton Halsey Thomas (New York, 1952), p. 264: entry of Oct. 8, 1862.

20. *New York Herald*, Oct. 1, 6, 11, 1862.
21. John G. Nicolay and John Hay, *Abraham Lincoln: A History*, 10 vols. (New York, 1890), 6: 157.
22. *The Collected Works of Abraham Lincoln*, ed. Roy P. Basler et al., 9 vols. (New Brunswick, N.J., 1953–1955), 5: 420.
23. Ibid., p. 434. Recognizing the historic nature of this occasion, both Gideon Welles and Salmon P. Chase made long entries in their diaries for September 22 describing the Cabinet meeting and quoting Lincoln directly and indirectly, from which this account is taken. *Diary of Gideon Welles*, ed. Howard K. Beale, 3 vols. (New York, 1960), 1: 142–45; *The Salmon P. Chase Papers, Vol. I: Journals, 1829–1872*, ed. John Niven (Kent, Ohio, 1993), pp. 393–95.
24. *O.R.*, ser. 1, vol. 24, pt. 3, p. 157.

25. *New York Tribune*, Sept. 23, 24, 1862; *Douglass' Monthly*, Oct. 1862, p. 721.
26. Gideon Welles, "The History of Emancipation," *The Galaxy* 14 (Dec. 1872): 846–47.
27. Porter to Manton Marble, Sept. 30, 1862, Marble Papers, Library of Congress, from the research notes of John Hennessy, used with permission.
28. McClellan to Ellen Marcy McClellan, Sept. 25, Oct. 5, 1862, McClellan Papers, Library of Congress; McClellan to William H. Aspinwall, Sept. 26, 1862, Civil War Collection, the Huntington Library; *O.R.*, ser. 1, vol. 19, pt. 2, pp. 395–96 — all items reprinted in *The Civil War Papers of George B. McClellan: Selected Correspondence, 1860–1865*, ed. Stephen W. Sears (New York, 1989), pp. 481–82, 489–90, 493–94.
29. *Springfield Republican*, Sept. 24, 1862; *Collected Works of Lincoln*, 5: 530.
30. John Slidell to James Mason, Oct. 2, 1862, enclosing parts of Shaftersbury's letter, quoted in Charles M. Hubbard, *The Failure of Confederate Diplomacy* (Knoxville, 1998), p. 117; *The Journal of Benjamin Moran* (Chicago, 1949), p. 1075: entry of Sept. 27, 1862.

31. *London Times*, Oct. 2, 1862.
32. Charles Francis Adams to Charles Francis Adams Jr., Oct. 17, 1862, in *A Cycle of Adams Letters 1861–1865*, ed. Worthington Chauncey Ford, 2 vols. (Boston, 1920), 1: 192; Charles Francis Adams to William H. Seward, Oct. 3, 1862, in *Papers Relating to Foreign Affairs, 1861–1862*, Part I (Washington, 1862), p. 205.
33. Ephraim Douglass Adams, *Great Britain and the American Civil War*, 2 vols. (New York, 1925), 2: 43–44, 54–55, reprints these two letters.
34. Palmerston to King Leopold, Nov. 18, 1862, quoted in Frank Merli and Theodore A. Wilson, "The British Cabinet and the Confederacy: Autumn, 1862," *Maryland Historical Magazine* 65 (1970): 261.
35. Mason to Judah Benjamin, Sept. 18, 1862, Mason to his son, Oct. 1, 1862, Mason to Benjamin, Nov. 7, 1862, in Virginia Mason, *The Public Life and Diplomatic Correspondence of James M. Mason* (New York, 1906), pp. 338, 342, 353–54.
36. Dayton to Seward, Oct. 14, 1862, *Papers Relating to Foreign Affairs, 1861–62*, 1: 394.

37. Chargé d'affaires quoted in Brian Jenkins, *Britain & the War for the Union*, 2 vols. (Montreal, 1974–1980), 2: 141; Russell quoted in Howard Jones, *Union in Peril: The Crisis over British Intervention in the Civil War* (Chapel Hill, N.C., 1992), p. 187.
38. Basler et al., eds., *Collected Works of Lincoln*, 5: 434.
39. *London Times*, Oct. 7, 1862.
40. *Glasgow Herald*, Oct. 10, 1862; *London Standard*, Oct. 7, 1862; *London Examiner*, Oct. 11, 1862; quoted in Alfred Grant, *The American Civil War and the British Press* (Jefferson, N.C., 2000), pp. 178, 29, and in Richard A. Heckman, "British Press Reaction to the Emancipation Proclamation," *Lincoln Herald* 71 (1969): 150. These studies quote several other newspapers to the same effect.
41. Dan Gow of Manchester quoted in Grant, *American Civil War and the British Press*, p. 32.
42. John Stuart Mill to John Lothrop Motley, late October 1862, printed in Henry Donaldson Jordan and Edwin J. Pratt, *Europe and the American Civil War* (Boston, 1931), p. 139; *Journal of Benjamin Moran*, p. 1077: entry of Oct. 6, 1862.

43. *London Morning Star,* Oct. 6, 1862, quoted in Allan Nevins, *The War for the Union, Vol. 2: War Becomes Revolution* (New York, 1960), p. 270.

44. Basler et al., eds., *Collected Works of Lincoln,* 6: 30.

45. *Christian Recorder,* Jan. 10, 1863.

46. *Journal of Benjamin Moran,* pp. 1107, 1110, 1115, 1161: entries of Jan. 16, 22, 30, May 13, 1863.

47. Henry Adams to Charles Francis Adams Jr., Jan. 23, 1863, in *The Letters of Henry Adams, Vol. 1: 1858–1868,* ed. J. C. Levenson (Cambridge, Mass., 1982), p. 327; Richard Cobden to Charles Sumner, Feb. 13, 1863, in *Europe Looks at the Civil War,* ed. Belle Becker Sideman and Lillian Friedman (New York, 1960), p. 222; James Shepherd Pike to William H. Seward, Dec. 31, 1862, quoted in Dean B. Mahin, *One War at a Time: The International Dimensions of the American Civil War* (Washington, 1999), p. 139.

48. Basler et al., eds., *Collected Works of Lincoln,* 5: 436–37.

49. Mark E. Neely Jr., *The Fate of Liberty: Abraham Lincoln and Civil Liberties* (New York, 1991), esp. Chap. 3.

50. Williston Lofton Jr., "Northern Labor

and the Negro during the Civil War," *Journal of Negro History* 34 (1949): 254; V. Jacque Voegeli, *Free But Not Equal: The Midwest and the Negro during the Civil War* (Chicago, 1967), p. 55.
51. *New York World*, Oct. 18, 1862; Seymour quoted in Nevins, *War Becomes Revolution*, p. 302n.
52. *New York Times*, Oct. 1, 1862.
53. Lyons to Lord John Russell, Nov. 17, 1862, in Nicolay and Hay, *Abraham Lincoln*, 6: 194 and n.
54. *New York Tribune*, Oct. 7, 1862.
55. *Richmond Enquirer*, Oct. 21, 31, 1862; *Richmond Examiner*, quoted in *New York Times*, Oct. 26, 1862.
56. *New York Times*, Oct. 8, 1862.
57. *The Tribune Almanac for 1861* (New York, 1861), p. 39; *The Tribune Almanac for 1863* (New York, 1863), p. 50.
58. *New York Times*, Oct. 16, 19, 1862.
59. *Diary of Gideon Welles*, 1: 169, 176: entries of Oct. 13, 18, 1862.
60. *New York Tribune*, Oct. 27, 1862; John Codman Ropes to John C. Gray, Nov. 9, in *War Letters of John Chipman and John C. Ropes, 1862–1865* (Boston, 1927), p. 19.

61. *O.R.*, ser. 1, vol. 19, pt. 1, p. 72; Basler et al., eds., *Collected Works of Lincoln*, 5: 474.

62. Lincoln to McClellan, Oct. 13, 1862, in Basler et al., eds., *Collected Works of Lincoln*, 5: 460–61.

63. Halleck to Hamilton R. Gamble, Oct. 30, 1862, in *O.R.*, ser. 3, vol. 2, pp. 703–4.

64. *Inside Lincoln's White House: The Complete Civil War Diary of John Hay*, ed. Michael Burlingame and John R. Turner Ettlinger (Carbondale, Ill., 1997), p. 232. Lincoln used the metaphor of a dull auger in a remark to Francis Preston Blair; see Blair to Montgomery Blair, Nov. 7, 1862, in William E. Smith, *The Francis Preston Blair Family in Politics*, 2 vols. (New York, 1933), 2: 144.

65. Bruce Catton, *Mr. Lincoln's Army* (Garden City, N.Y., 1951), pp. 334–36; William F. Keeler to Anna Keeler, Nov. 9, 1864, in *Aboard the USS Florida, 1863–1865: The Letters of Paymaster William F. Keeler*, ed. Robert W. Daly (Annapolis, Md., 1968), p. 200.

66. *The Diary of George Templeton Strong*, p. 271; Peter J. Parish, *The American Civil War* (New York, 1975), pp. 208–

9; Joel H. Silbey, *A Respectable Minority: The Democratic Party in the Civil War Era, 1860–1868* (New York, 1977), p. 144.

67. *The Tribune Almanac for 1863* (New York, 1863) contains the most complete data on the 1862 elections.

68. Calculated from ibid.

69. Daly, *Diary of a Union Lady*, p. 333: entry of Jan. 19, 1865, recounting a conversation with Hancock the previous evening; James Longstreet, "The Invasion of Maryland," in *Battles and Leaders of the Civil War*, ed. Clarence C. Buel and Robert U. Johnson, 4 vols. (New York, 1888), 2: 674. Hancock was still a brigade commander at Antietam.

Bibliographical Essay

Although the principal sources for this book were contemporary newspapers, official documents and correspondence, personal letters, diaries, and memoirs of soldiers, political leaders, diplomats, and ordinary citizens, and miscellaneous primary sources, this bibliographical essay is confined mainly to books and articles that the reader interested in pursuing various themes in greater detail may wish to consult. The citation endnotes constitute a guide to the primary sources.

BIOGRAPHIES. The number of biographies of Abraham Lincoln seems almost infinite. For the events covered in this book, the most useful one-volume biographies are David Herbert Donald, *Lincoln* (New York, 1995), Benjamin P. Thomas, *Abraham Lincoln* (New York, 1952), Stephen B. Oates, *With Malice Toward None: The Life of Abraham Lincoln* (New York, 1977), and Mark E. Neely Jr., *The Last Best Hope of Earth: Abraham Lincoln and the Promise of*

America (Cambridge, Mass., 1993). The relevant volumes of two multivolume biographies are also invaluable: John G. Nicolay and John Hay, *Abraham Lincoln: A History*, 10 vols. (New York, 1890), vols. 5 and 6, and James G. Randall, *Lincoln the President*, 4 vols. (New York, 1946–1955), vol. 2. For Jefferson Davis the two best biographies are William J. Cooper Jr., *Jefferson Davis, American* (New York, 2000) and William C. Davis, *Jefferson Davis: The Man and His Hour* (New York, 1991). For the principal Union army commanders, see Stephen W. Sears, *George B. McClellan: The Young Napoleon* (New York, 1988), Thomas J. Rowland, *George B. McClellan and Civil War History* (Kent, Ohio, 1998), Wallace J. Schutz and Walter N. Trenerry, *Abandoned By Lincoln: A Military Biography of General John Pope* (Urbana, Ill., 1990), and Peter Cozzens, *General John Pope: A Life for the Nation* (Urbana, Ill., 2000). An interesting perspective can be found in William Marvel, *Burnside* (Chapel Hill, N.C., 1991). The number of Robert E. Lee biographies is second only to those of Lincoln. The most important are Douglas Southall Freeman, *R. E. Lee: A Biography*, 4 vols. (New York, 1934–1935) and Emory M. Thomas, *Robert E. Lee: A Biography* (New York, 1995). See also Gary W. Gallagher, ed., *Lee the Soldier* (Lincoln, Neb., 1996). The actions of Jackson and Longstreet are narrated in James I. Robertson Jr., *Stonewall Jackson: The Man, the Soldier, the Legend* (New York, 1997) and Jeffry D. Wert, *General James Longstreet* (New York, 1993).

MILITARY BACKGROUND AND CONTEXT OF THE ANTIETAM CAMPAIGN. Nearly a half-century after its initial publication, Shelby Foote's *The Civil War: A Narrative: Fort Sumter to Perryville* (New York, 1958) still stands as the most complete and readable military narrative of the war's first eighteen months. Classics of equal stature treating the Army of Northern Virginia and Army of the Potomac are Douglas Southall Freeman, *Lee's Lieutenants: Manassas to Malvern Hill* (New York, 1942) and *Lee's Lieutenants: Cedar Mountain to Chancellorsville* (New York, 1943) and Bruce Catton, *Mr. Lincoln's Army* (Garden City, N.Y., 1951). See also the 1862 section of George Walsh, *Damage Them All You Can: Robert E. Lee's Army of Northern Virginia* (New York, 2002). Many important insights can be found in T. Harry Williams, *Lincoln and His Generals* (New York, 1952), Steven E. Woodworth, *Davis and Lee at War* (Lawrence, Kans., 1995), Gabor S. Boritt, ed., *Lincoln's Generals* (New York, 1994), and Boritt, ed., *Jefferson Davis's Generals* (New York, 1999).

The Peninsula Campaign, the Seven Days Battles, and the Second Battle of Manassas/Bull Run are superbly narrated and analyzed in the following books: Stephen W. Sears, *To the Gates of Richmond: The Peninsula Campaign* (New York, 1992), Gary W. Gallagher, ed., *The Richmond Campaign of 1862* (Chapel Hill, N.C., 2000), and John J. Hennessy, *Return to Bull Run: The Campaign and Battle of Second Manassas* (New York, 1993). For the evolution of Lee's strategic thinking through these campaigns, consult Joseph L. Harsh, *Confederate Tide Rising: Robert E. Lee and the Making of Southern Strategy* (Kent, Ohio, 1998).

THE INVASION OF MARYLAND AND THE BATTLE OF ANTIETAM. For a valuable bibliography of primary and secondary sources, see D. Scott Hartwig, *The Battle of Antietam and the Maryland Campaign of 1862: A Bibliography* (Westport, Conn., 1990). Two superb narratives of Antietam, which cover the invasion of Maryland, the capture of Harpers Ferry, and the South

Mountain battles as well as Antietam, have achieved the status of classics: James V. Murfin, *The Gleam of Bayonets: The Battle of Antietam and Robert E. Lee's Maryland Campaign, September 1862* (Baton Rouge, La., 1965) and Stephen W. Sears, *Landscape Turned Red: The Battle of Antietam* (New Haven, Conn., 1983). An exhaustive study of Confederate strategy and leadership in this campaign is likely also to become a classic: Joseph L. Harsh, *Taken at the Flood: Robert E. Lee and Confederate Strategy in the Maryland Campaign of 1862* (Kent, Ohio, 1999). For some of the documentation on which this book is based, plus additional data, see also Harsh, *Sounding the Shallows: A Confederate Companion for the Maryland Campaign of 1862* (Kent, Ohio, 2000). John Michael Priest, *Before Antietam: The Battle for South Mountain* (New York, 1992) and Priest, *Antietam: The Soldiers' Battle* (Shippensburg, Pa., 1989) are microhistories with many detailed maps that enable the reader to follow the actions of nearly every regiment on both sides. The reader may not be convinced by the argument of Paul R. Teetor, *A Matter of Hours: Treason at Harper's Ferry* (Rutherford, N.J., 1982) that Col. Dixon Miles deliberately betrayed Harpers Ferry to the enemy, but will learn a great deal about the siege. Perry D. Jamieson, *Death in September: The Antietam Campaign* (Fort Worth, Tex., 1995), contains a brief narrative of the campaign and battle plus useful capsule biographies of the leading participants. The essays in Gary W. Gallagher, ed., *Antietam: Essays on the 1862 Maryland Campaign* (Kent, Ohio, 1989) and Gallagher, ed., *The Antietam Campaign* (Chapel Hill, N.C., 1999) represent the very best scholarship on various facets of the campaign and battle. Finally, William A. Frassanito, *Antietam: The Photographic Legacy of America's Bloodiest Day* (New York, 1976) contains the best-known photographs of the battlefield by Alexander Gardner and James Gibson and astute commentary on their impact, along with modern photographs taken at the same spots and with the same camera angles as the historic photographs.

THE POLITICAL CONTEXT. The biographies of Lincoln and Davis cited in the biography section, above, include a great deal of material on this theme. The best single account of politics and government policies in both the Union and Confederacy, as well as military and other developments in 1862, is Allan Nevins, *The War for the Union, Vol. 2:*

War Becomes Revolution (New York, 1960). See also chs. 15–18 of James M. McPherson, *Battle Cry of Freedom: The Civil War Era* (New York, 1988). Other studies containing important information and insights on Northern politics in 1862, including the congressional elections (no important elections occurred that year in the Confederacy), are Bruce Tap, *Over Lincoln's Shoulder: The Committee on the Conduct of the War* (Lawrence, Kans., 1998), Hans L. Trefousse, *The Radical Republicans: Lincoln's Vanguard for Racial Justice* (New York, 1969), Christopher Dell, *Lincoln and the War Democrats* (Rutherford, N.J., 1975), Wood Gray, *The Hidden Civil War: The Story of the Copperheads* (New York, 1942), and George Fort Milton, *Abraham Lincoln and the Fifth Column* (New York, 1962).

THE PRESS AND PUBLIC OPINION. Newspapers both shaped and reflected public morale through their reporting and editorial commentary. The Northern press, the four major New York papers in particular (*Herald*, *Tribune*, *Times*, and *World*), sent top-flight reporters to the battle fronts. The Richmond newspapers did as much as they could with limited resources to get correspondents to the front, but they could not match the Northern output. There are several worthwhile books on the Civil War press; see especially J. Cutler Andrews, *The North Reports the Civil War* (Pittsburgh, 1955) and *The South Reports the Civil War* (Princeton, N.J., 1970), Louis M. Starr, *Reporting the Civil War* (New York, 1962), Brayton Harris, *Blue and Gray in Black & White: Newspapers in the Civil War* (Washington, 1999), Emmet Crozier, *Yankee Reporters, 1861–1865* (New York, 1956), Bernard A. Weisberger, *Reporters for the Union* (Boston, 1953), Eric T. Dean Jr., " 'We Live under a Government of Men and Morning Newspapers': Image, Expectation, and the Peninsula Campaign of 1862," *Virginia Magazine of History and Biography* 103 (1995): 5–28, and James M. McPherson, " 'Spend Much Time in Reading the Daily Papers': The Press and Army Morale in the Civil War," *Atlanta History* 42 (1998): 7–18. In addition, biographies of the Big Four of New York journalism in this era are useful: Ralph R. Fahrney, *Horace Greeley and the Tribune in the Civil War* (Cedar Rapids, Iowa, 1936), Oliver Carlson, *The Man Who Made the News: James Gordon Bennett* (New York, 1942), Francis Brown, *Raymond of the Times* (New York, 1951), and George T. McJimsey, *Genteel Partisan:*

Manton Marble, 1834–1917 (Ames, Iowa, 1971).

THE EMANCIPATION ISSUE. This important question is treated in most of the works cited in the section on politics above. In addition, see John Hope Franklin, *The Emancipation Proclamation* (Garden City, N.Y., 1963), Hans L. Trefousse, ed., *Lincoln's Decision for Emancipation* (Philadelphia, 1975), Benjamin Quarles, *Lincoln and the Negro* (New York, 1962), James M. McPherson, *Abraham Lincoln and the Second American Revolution* (New York, 1991), Michael Vorenberg, *Final Freedom: The Civil War, the Abolition of Slavery, and the Thirteenth Amendment,* ch. 1 (New York, 2001), Ira Berlin et al., *Slaves No More,* ch. 1 (Cambridge, Mass., 1992), and James M. McPherson, "Who Freed the Slaves?" in McPherson, *Drawn with the Sword: Reflections on the American Civil War* (New York, 1996), pp. 192–207. The opposition to emancipation in the North on racist grounds is analyzed in V. Jacque Voegeli, *Free but Not Equal: The Midwest and the Negro during the Civil War* (Chicago, 1967) and Forrest G. Wood, *Black Scare: The Racist Response to Emancipation and Reconstruction* (Berkeley, Calif., 1968).

★ ★ ★

FOREIGN POLICY. D. P. Crook, *The North, the South, and the Powers, 1861–1865* (New York, 1974) and Henry Donaldson Jordan and Edwin J. Pratt, *Europe and the American Civil War* (Boston, 1931) provide an introduction to this issue. See also Charles M. Hubbard, *The Failure of Confederate Diplomacy* (Knoxville, 1998) and Dean M. Mahin, *One War at a Time: The International Dimensions of the American Civil War* (Washington, 1999). There is a large and rich literature on Anglo-American and Anglo-Confederate relations. Much of it concentrates on the crucial issue of diplomatic recognition of the Confederacy in 1862. The two classic studies are Ephraim D. Adams, *Great Britain and the American Civil War*, 2 vols. (New York, 1925) and Frank L. Owsley, *King Cotton Diplomacy: Foreign Relations of the Confederate States of America*, 2nd ed., rev. by Harriet C. Owsley (Chicago, 1959). Other important works include Brian Jenkins, *Britain and the War for the Union*, 2 vols. (Montreal, 1974, 1980), Howard Jones, *Union in Peril: The Crisis over British Intervention in the Civil War* (Chapel Hill, N.C., 1992), Kinley J. Brauer, "British Mediation and the American Civil War," *Journal of Southern History* 38 (1972): 49–

335

64, Edward E. Ellsworth, "Anglo-American Affairs in October of 1862," *Lincoln Herald* 66 (1964): 89–96, and Frank Merli and Theodore A. Wilson, "The British Cabinet and the Confederacy: Autumn, 1862," *Maryland Historical Magazine* 65 (1970): 239–62. Most of these studies deal in some degree with British public opinion; for works that focus mainly on that matter, see R. J. M. Blackett, *Divided Hearts: Britain and the American Civil War* (Baton Rouge, La., 2001) and Alfred Grant, *The American Civil War and the British Press* (London, 2000).

Next to Britain, France was the most important foreign power involved in Civil War diplomacy. Lynn M. Case and Warren F. Spencer, *The United States and France: Civil War Diplomacy* (Philadelphia, 1970) is a thorough study; it can be supplemented by Daniel B. Carroll, *Henri Mercier and the American Civil War* (Princeton, N.J., 1971). George M. Blackburn, *French Newspaper Opinion on the American Civil War* (Westport, Conn., 1997) is disappointing.

The critical role of the slavery issue in Civil War diplomacy is the main focus of Howard Jones, *Abraham Lincoln and the New Birth of Freedom* (Lincoln, Neb.,

1999). See also Douglas A. Lorimer, "The Role of Anti-Slavery Sentiment in English Reactions to the American Civil War," *Historical Journal* 19 (1976): 405–20, Kinley J. Brauer, "The Slavery Problem in the Diplomacy of the American Civil War," *Pacific Historical Review* 46 (Aug. 1977): 439–69, and James M. McPherson, " 'The Whole Family of Man': Lincoln and the Last Best Hope Abroad," in McPherson, *Drawn with the Sword: Reflections on the American Civil War* (New York, 1996), pp. 208–27.

Acknowledgments

A scholar's foremost debt is to the libraries and archives whence comes the raw material for a book. I did most of the research for this book at the Firestone Library of Princeton University, whose resources on the American Civil War are excellent. The collections in the library of Antietam National Battlefield also immeasurably enriched the book; I am especially grateful to Ted Alexander, chief historian at Antietam National Battlefield, for his guidance in using these collections. To John Hennessy, assistant superintendent of Fredericksburg-Spotsylvania National Military Park and an outstanding historian as well, I owe a debt of gratitude beyond my power to express for his generosity in sharing his research notes on the Army of the Potomac. Nicholas Picerno of Claremont, New Hampshire, kindly gave me permission to quote from a letter in his possession written by Captain George H. Nye of the 10th Maine. Manuscript collections at the Library of Congress, the Huntington Library, the Illinois

State Historical Library, and the Western Reserve Historical Society also provided important material; I thank the staffs of these repositories for their assistance.

David Hackett Fischer, my co-editor of the series of which this volume is a part, Pivotal Moments in American History, and our editor at Oxford University Press, Peter Ginna, read the manuscript and improved it greatly with their suggestions, as did Jennifer Weber, a graduate student at Princeton University. I greatly appreciate their help. Joellyn Ausanka at Oxford University Press expertly shepherded the manuscript through the publication process. To my wife, Patricia McPherson, I express my greatest thanks, and my love, for her work as a research assistant, proofreading partner, and partner for life.

The employees of Thorndike Press hope you have enjoyed this Large Print book. All our Thorndike and Wheeler Large Print titles are designed for easy reading, and all our books are made to last. Other Thorndike Press Large Print books are available at your library, through selected bookstores, or directly from us.

For information about titles, please call:

(800) 223-1244

or visit our Web site at:

www.gale.com/thorndike
www.gale.com/wheeler

To share your comments, please write:

Publisher
Thorndike Press
295 Kennedy Memorial Drive
Waterville, ME   04901